"We are not human beings on a spiritual journey. We are spiritual beings on a human journey."
Stephen R. Covey

Copyright Page

Published in the United States, First Edition, 2024

Cover Design by: Dineen Miller

ISBN 979-8-9898684-0-7
Library of Congress Control Number 2024900994

Other books by this author:

- ➢ *Ilion My Childhood My Memories – Growing Up in a By-Gone Era*
- ➢ *My Rosemount MN. Memories – Teenage Years in My Shoes*

Dedication

The question of what happens to us when we die, and what lies beyond the 'Veil' has been debated for millenniums.

Many people think that when a loved one dies – that's it. That person is now gone forever, gone to the afterlife, and we won't hear from them again until we die. Well maybe that is not really the case.

Have you had experiences or as I call them, **Signs**, that really made you think, rethink and challenge your beliefs about a person's death and the afterlife? You're not alone!

Through unlocking and discovering the meaning of these Signs, the conscience can further process its relevance to our lives. Through further discernment one can bring understanding and perhaps needed directional change at a most opportune time.

This book is dedicated to those of you who relish exploring the unknown, the desire to know the meaning of what you have or are experiencing, and the daring to question it all. It is with perseverance to that discovery of understanding that drives the curious souls onward.

Michael Smith, a blogger and friend writes: "*In my life, one thing I have learned is that science is insufficient to explain the universe. It seems the math gets to a point where the explainable becomes unexplained. All these equations eventually get to 'and then something happened' point where they become insufficient. Religion shares a similar deficiency for people who demand hard proof, largely because religion requires faith, a belief in the unexplainable. It seems to me that we need both science and religion to explain our place in the grand scheme of things."*

This book contains a collection of true stories, each linked to a theme of how the Veil is thinner than we imagine. I truly hope that this book enlightens you, the reader, and further engages you in your own self exploration.

As Leonard Nimoy was quoted saying, *"This is the exploration that awaits you! Not mapping stars and studying nebula, but charting the unknown possibilities of existence."*

And finally, from Aaron Mahnke author of: *The World of Lore* series; speaker, and podcaster has stated "The afterlife, the *other world, whatever we want to call it, it's right there. We just need to reach beyond the Veil."*

SIGNS: The Veil Is Thinner Than We Imagine!

Table of Contents

INTRODUCTION

Have you experienced something that you cannot logically explain such as: a sound, a smell, a movement, a feeling of being touched or directed, perhaps an unexpected visit by one of nature's creatures such as a bird, a butterfly or other animal?

Have you had dreams of a departed loved one that were so extremely vivid and real or lifelike and that the dream left you with a feeling of comfort and/or wellbeing? Have you thought that it was all a coincidence? Are you looking for answers to why strange occurrences happen in your life?

This book is about what I have termed – **Signs,** but not just any signs, ones that have special meaning by offering through their interpretation, a message for the receiver of the sign.

As the **Five** *Man Electrical Band's song goes – Sign, sign everywhere a sign...* The signs that the band were referring to were street signs, building signs, store front signs, and those that are all around us and manage to direct, guide, caution, inform, and alert us. Those signs are ubiquitous, but the Signs this book will be addressing are the more subtle ones, the personal ones, the ones that might come from a dream, a passing word, a touch or a gentle nudge, a visit by a woodland creature, an unexpected gesture, an object's unprovoked movement, or even a 'timed' breeze on an otherwise calm day. Something you might have

i

described as perhaps other-worldly. These **Signs** let us know that we are not alone, that indeed the **Veil is thinner than we imagine**.

You might recall in the movie *Tommy Boy, staring Chris Farley* – at the end of the movie Tommy Boy is in a small sail boat on a pond and it's a real calm day. He's sitting in the boat and talking out loud to his deceased father when he realizes he's late to meet his girlfriend, and all of a sudden out of nowhere the wind comes up and blows the sailboat towards shore. For the sake of this book, and for Tommy Boy, that timed breeze would be interpretated as a **Sign.**

Within this book I describe the experiences of the Signs that myself and others have had and how those experiences were received and interpreted. Where possible, I present you with the necessary background information to validate these Signs, or further question their meaning.

This is perhaps the most challenging book I have ever undertaken, for how can one tell other's stories while adequately capturing the mysterious and fleeting messages which left them wondering what happened? Some of their 'signs' meanings were immediately known, while others took some thought and time to discern. Each Sign with its own story to tell, a unique message to impart. I have attempted to relay those messages with clarity and their feelings with emotion, hoping that they may offer insight into the mysteries of life's direction.

I recently read an article titled: ***Olivia Newton-John's Family Talks 'Supernatural' Encounters with Late Star in Year After Her Death,*** written by Katie Jerkovich Aug 9, 2023, for DailyWire.com. The article goes on to describe Olivia Newton-John's loved ones reflecting upon the first anniversary of her death and discussing what they described as "supernatural" encounters with the late star.

> *Chloe, Olivia's daughter stated that "Mom and I had talked years back. We'd watch these paranormal shows, and I'd say, you gotta show up for me. And she was like, I'll show up as one of those orb things."*
> *"Two weeks after she passed my phone accidentally took a picture of my dog, and there floating by his head was a little blue orb, the same color as this,".* (The 'This' she referred to was the Aquamarine stone in the pendent she was wearing).

Additionally, Chloe mentioned that she has felt her mom's "wings" wrap around her and give her needed encouragement.

These are some of the various Signs I will be discussing through the telling of several individuals' stories. And as I tell these stories I wish to challenge you to think about what this all means:

- Is it past loved ones letting us know they are still here?
- Is it proof that we do not pass into nothingness?
- Is it proof that there is a greater power?
- Is it proof that we are all connected in the cosmos?
- Is it guardian angels, or otherwise spiritual in nature?
- Is it nothing more than coincidence or our imagination?

Please Note: I am in no way describing, insinuating or offering any form of the occult, or anything of a demonic or dark nature, nor any of its learnings, etc... Furthermore, I do not entertain any discussion of it along with my presentation of material within this book.

By telling these stories I invite you to be open to the potential of Signs that may be happening around you, signs you may already be receiving. I invite you to look for their meaning, and maybe embrace the messages that these Signs are presenting. These Signs may have some logical reason for occurring when and where they did, but without further examination of their occurrence, one is only left with the wonder of that '**what just happened**' feeling.

I know I'm not the only one who has experienced these sometimes unexplainable events. Others have made me aware of their experiences, and some of them have allowed me to present their stories within this book. Still others have told me that they'd like to block it out of their mind for various reasons.

I hope that by discussing these personal experiences, that it may cause you to begin to question your own potential experiences; to begin your journey of exploration by taking the necessary steps to acknowledge, to understand and maybe even to accept the meaning of your own Sign experiences. Further by presenting these Sign stories, and comments from noted experts, it is my hope that the overall stigma of having such events can be diminished and replaced with acceptance of the messages that are often presented with the experience.

There is tremendous power in the acknowledgement of the SIGNS that are presented to you. They should not be feared or ignored, but pursued for the understanding and the meaning they may have in your life.

Therefore, it is my wish that this book brings you further acknowledgement, understanding, acceptance, peace and comfort for the Signs that you may already be experiencing.

"The most beautiful thing we can experience, is the mysterious. It is the source of all true art and science."
Albert Einstein

Let us begin our journey together.

So we fix our eyes not on what is seen, but on what is unseen, since what is unseen is eternal. 2 Corinthians 4:18

BOOK DESIGN AND LAYOUT

There is a purposeful design to the layout of this book. The SIGNS I will present can come in many different methods of delivery. As example the Signs could be received from objects, through dreams, through your asking for them, from the animal world or via the interaction with numbers. Knowing this I have decided to organize this book into sections – each representing a theme and the stories that depict the theme are then overviewed within the chapters contained within that section.

Therefore, the Sign stories will be divided into five (5) main sections. These sections will be based upon the method or means by which the Sign was received. Within each section will be chapters demonstrating the section heading. Those Sections will be as follows:

> **Grouping One: Directed Intervention**
> **Grouping Two: End of Life and Visitation Dreams**
> **Grouping Three: Objects and Smells**
> **Grouping Four: Asking for Help**
> **Grouping Five: Animals and Numbers**

And just like a 'Patchwork Quilt', these stories all stitch together through the presenting of the Signs that enabled the reader to not only understand the message, but to also understand that Signs can be sent and received in many varying ways.

1 GROUPING ONE: DIRECTED INTERVENTION

Have you experienced a whispered voice when no one's around, or a gentle nudge appearing to direct you, or having a vision so real that it left an undeniable impression upon you?

Within this section are stories of Signs that highlight what I refer to as a direct intervention, what some might call a spiritual intervention, and still others might refer to them as the Third Person Factor. These signs are most definitely personal, and done to directly influence or guide the recipient, and might be received in order to prevent harm to the recipient, or to bring safety, comfort, relief and even joy.

1.1 9/11 TWIN TOWERS TRAGEDY, MIRACULOUS ESCAPES AND WE MUST NEVER FORGET!

The September 11 attacks, commonly known as 9/11, were four coordinated suicide terrorist attacks carried out by al-Qaeda against the United States in 2001. That morning, 19 terrorists hijacked four commercial airliners scheduled to travel from the New England and Mid-Atlantic regions of the East Coast to California. The hijackers crashed the first two planes into the Twin Towers of the World Trade Center in New York City, two of the world's tallest buildings at the time, the other two hijacked planes were aimed toward targets in or near Washington, D.C., in an attack on the nation's capital. The third plane succeeded in crashing into the Pentagon, the headquarters of the U.S. Department of Defense in Arlington County, Virginia, while the fourth plane crashed in rural Pennsylvania following a passenger revolt. These attacks killed nearly 3,000 people and instigated the multi-decade global war on terror. – Wikipedia September 11 Attacks

Like most of us, I was working that day. At 8:46 AM the first plane, American Airlines flight 11, hit the north tower of the Twin Towers in New York City. Shortly thereafter the second plane hit the south tower. The news of this spread quickly through our offices.

Xerox, the company I worked for then, had employees and a large printing center in the North Tower, tower 1 of the Twin Towers. The employees working in the print center that day all managed to exit the buildings prior to their collapse. However, as we grievously learned many others within those buildings were not as fortunate.

Brian Clarke and Ron DiFrancesco, are survivors of the tragedy that unfolded that day at the Twin Towers. The following are their stories of the horrific events that happened, and how they managed, with perhaps some divine intervention, to make it out alive. And while cautiously making their way out of the building, they managed to also rescue another person named Stanley Praimnath.

To help with the next two stories you might want to refer to this visual. WTC1 was the North Tower and WTC2 was the South Tower. Photo from Wikipedia.
http://en.turkcewiki.org/wiki/September_11_attacks

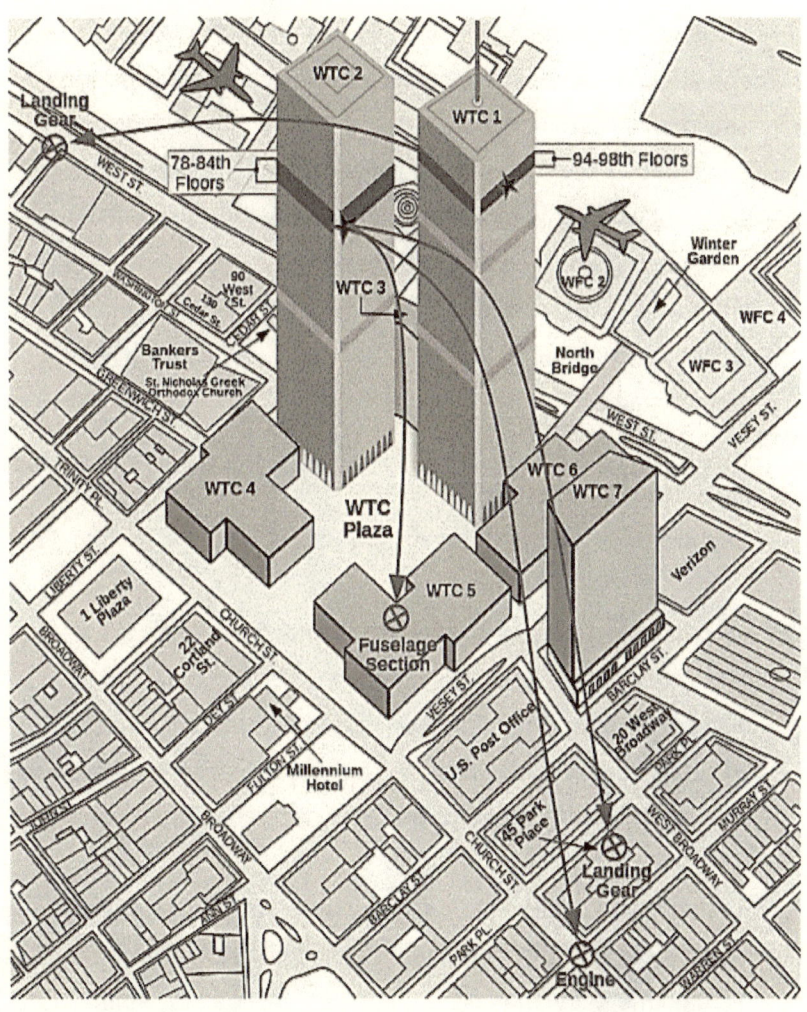

Brian Clark's 9/11 Story:

Brian Clark worked on the 84th floor of the South Tower, was the Executive Vice President for Euro Brokers, and also an office Fire Marshall. At 9:03AM United Airlines flight 175 crashed into the South Tower impacting floors 77 – 85.

While doing research for this book, I came across Brian's story and began listening to his media interviews. I feel I was being drawn to his personal story in a way that I can't really describe. The reason I say that is that each year since the tragic events of 9/11, not wanting to relive that painful time, I have stayed away from viewing any media on the anniversary. Painfully as a result of the events that unfolded that day, we saw 2977 victims perish at the hands of the 19 hijackers, who also died committing murder-suicide.

https://en.wikipedia.org/wiki/
Casualties_of_the_September_11_attacks

As Brian describes the events that unfolded next, he said fear came over him as the building swayed from the impact of the plane. However, when the building settled back to its vertical position, as Brian describes: "the fear I was feeling vanished and a sense of '**you're going to be OK**' washed over me".

Brian's story intrigued me. His description of the events he experienced that day after the building came back to vertical, directed me to try and connect with him. I began my searching via social media (SM) and I soon found where he was working.

Reaching out to his place of employment, my hope was that they would pass the message along to him.

After a few weeks of waiting for a response, I again went back to SM and decided to use LinkedIn and see if he was profiled there, and finding he was I sent him a friend request with a message of introduction. After a few email exchanges Brian and I arranged for a time to speak.

Friday March 17, 2023 Brian and I met over the phone. During the call, and after introducing myself to Brian I proceeded to describe this book I was writing and why I was so anxious to meet with him. I also stated that I did not want to cause him any more stress by asking him to recount that horrific day's events. Brian's response was that he was fine with talking about his experience of that day, and with that we began our talk.

Brian's story reads almost like a made for Hollywood movie, with him being the hero, and that despite all odds, he manages to make it out alive. Well, it wasn't a movie, but his experiences that day do tell of heroism, intestinal fortitude and determination. But also have what is for me through the telling of his story, Signs that he was assisted that day, assistance that may have come from something beyond the veil.

After the second airplane had hit the south tower, with his floor destroyed, scattered with debris and the lights going out, being on his company's 'fire safety team', Brian grabbed for his flashlight and whistle from his desk. "I Immediately began flashing the light around and soon I was joined by six (6) other people from my floor who had made their way through the debris and over to me".

Brian then led this group to the hallway in the center of the building, where the hallway offered several stairwell choices A, B, and C, as well as the elevators which were definitely not operational. Brian stated: "my instinct was to head towards stairwell C, and as I began to move towards that stairwell, I received a push on my right shoulder as if directing me towards stairwell A. Looking around to see who was pushing me, I found no one there". And as he described it: "Oh well stairwell A will be fine too." Later he found out that stairwell A was the only stairwell clear enough of debris to allow people to traverse it.

Brian then proceeded to lead the group down stairwell A, until at the 81st floor landing, they were met by two people coming up the stairs. The people coming up stated that there was fire, smoke and debris below and that they should proceed upwards to the roof. While the group debated which way to go, Brian heard a muffled sound coming from inside the room next to the stairwell. As Brian described it: "I heard a person cry out for help – that he was trapped."

The impact of the plane had caused the locked 81st floor doorframe to partially come away from the drywall. Brian and another man, his co-worker Ron DiFrancesco were able to rip away enough drywall to create a large enough opening to slip through and soon they were inside the 81st floor.

"Using my flashlight, I began to direct the beam towards the sound and saw what was most certainly a hand waving from a man trapped." Ron (much more on Ron later), at this point found it very difficult to breath in the intense smoke that surrounded the area, and so he went back to the stairwell, leaving Brian and the stranger alone. Interestingly Brian stated: "at that moment I had felt like I had a bubble of fresh air all around me".

Turning his attention to locating the person calling out for help, Brian soon found him trapped behind a wall that was separating the two of them. "Looking around I found a desk and stood it up on its end at the wall. I began to climb up so that I could look over the wall to the other side."

"I saw the person, who had been trapped, now reaching up towards me. I encouraging him to jump, and when he did, I grabbed onto him and with giving it all the strength I had, I was able to pull the man up and over the wall that was between us. At that point the desk tipped over and we both tumbled back onto the floor, landing one on top of the other. We then both quickly rose and introduced themselves." The man that Brian rescued that day was Stanley Praimnath. (By the way, both men discuss to this day, or perhaps argue, as to who really saved whom.)

Brian and Stanley, now needing to get out of the building, looked back towards the doorway and the stairs. Once back at the stairwell landing, they found that all of the others, including Ron DiFrancesco, were now gone perhaps deciding to go up the

7

stairs in hopes of finding cleaner air and rescue from the roof top. However, that is not the direction these two men decided upon going. For some odd reason, as Brian describes it: "I still felt very calm knowing that both I and Stanley would be ok."

Brian and Stanley walked down the stairs and for a while they saw no other person, then around the 68th floor they came upon one man heading up the stairs. Jose Marrero, a co-worker of Brian's, was heading up to help out others that he heard call out on his walkie talkie in need of help. Brian cautioned Jose to rethink his efforts and to go with them, but Jose said no that he needed to help the others. Needless to say, Jose, in trying to help others get to safety, did not make it out of the building alive.

Brian and Stanley made it out of the building at about 9:50AM and away from the area walking down Church Street until they came upon the backside of Trinity Church where two priests were standing outside. The four of them began to talk and the priests asked if Brian and Stanley would have prayer with them, which they all then proceeded to do. The priests then stated that the church was open and proceeded to invite them inside if they wanted to, and as they walked up Rector Street to go to the church entrance, they looked back at the towers with Stanley stating he felt that the tower was going to come down.

They stood there as if being directed to watch, as the South Tower, the very building they had come out of, was now crumbling to the ground. Ash from the building began flying everywhere as Brian and Stanley ran south on Broadway, and

8

with the wave of ash almost upon them, they entered 42 Broadway to take cover, and stayed there for around 45 minutes. Unbeknownst to them, the North Tower had imploded at 10:30AM.

Fifteen minutes later they exited the back door of 42 Broadway and somehow at that time Stanley and Brian got separated from one another. Interestingly neither of them can tell you how that actually happened.

Brian, now alone, continued walking towards the East River and as he passed Pier 11, he heard an announcement from the pier operator that the next ferry was leaving for New Jersey. As he recalls: "the ferry does not typically leave from that pier and head to Jersey City, but needless to say I ran down to the pier and made it onboard the ferry just as the gate closed behind me."

Well, that's not the end of Brian's story – he successfully made it to Jersey City where he found a working phone and called home to let his family know that he was OK and that he would manage to get himself to Hoboken where he would then catch a train to his car and drive home. By the way this phone call home shocked his family as they were under the belief that Brian did not make it out of the building in time before the collapse. To find out more as to why the family thought that, Brian's YouTube video of his presentation at Mesquite ISD school A 9/11 Survivors Story explains that in detail.

"After a forty-minute walk north to the Hoboken train station I had arrived. I then heard a public address announcement that my train had been delayed and would now be departing in five minutes. And at that point, I felt like the train was purposefully held up just for me".

At the end of the fifty-minute train ride, Brian walked to his car and drove home where he was reunited with his family. As he pulled into his driveway with the car horn blaring, as he describes it: "There was a love fest right there on my front lawn with my family and friends just enveloping me."

Yet once again that is not the end of Brian's story and his Signs. One week later Brian was sleeping and had a dream where Jose Marrero, the person who had passed Brian and Stanley on the stairwell, came to him and stood at the foot of his bed. Brian stated: "I could see Jose plain as day and he was wearing a very bright white, almost glowing billowy shirt. I could only see the top half of Jose as the foot of my bed blocked Jose's lower body." Brian immediately said "Jose, you are OK, how'd you do it. Jose looked at me with a big smile on his face and nodded, and at that moment I not only understood that Jose was dead, but that he was also OK and that my other office mates, who had also perished that day were OK too. And at that point I woke up".

I have related here, as best I could, the conversation that Brian and I had on the phone. We discussed the meaning of a higher power intervening that day. Brian further mentioned a book he had read called 'The Third Man Factor' (by John Geiger). In this book the Third Man is described as an unseen 'being' that intervenes at a critical moment — when people are in great stress or in a life-and-death struggle, and they become present in order to give comfort, aid, guidance and support. The Third Man has often been described as a spiritual presence or even a guardian Angel. Brian did mention that when he and Stanley got separated, he thought that perhaps Stanley might actually have been an illusion, a third man, perhaps a guardian angel.

Brian is now retired and lives a fulfilling life with his family, friends and with the occasional retelling of his and Stanley's story of that day. As he so often says, 'Every day is a great day, some are just greater than others.' He also reminds us through his public talks, to not dwell on the past, do not over plan for the future – instead live in the present. By the way, Brian and Stanley have remained best of friends as a result of their 9/11 experience.

Thank you, Brian for allowing me to retell your story and to bring to light the many Signs I think you had that day. Either consciously or sub-consciously you listened to and comprehended the various signs, and as a result you and Stanley made it out alive.

Recapping Brian and Stanley's event from that day the Signs that I see that presented themselves began with Brian leading the group of office mates to the stairwell where **he felt a push on his right shoulder** directing him to stairwell A. This then enabled Brian to help rescue Stanley. Then there was **the**

mysterious air bubble that appeared around him in the smoke filled 81st floor, and even when he and Stanley were at Trinity Church and the ash from the tower collapse filled the air – Brian stated that he felt that fresh air bubble around him then too.

The next sign was **the ferry leaving for Jersey**, from an area of the Hudson that it normally doesn't leave from, and **Brian making it onboard just before the gate closed.** That was followed by his walking to the train station in Hoboken **where the train had been delayed, just long enough,** thereby allowing Brian to make it onto the train in time. Then one week later Brian having had the **'Visitation Dream' with Jose** and the unsaid message Brian took from that.

For me these are all Signs that aided Brian during that horrific event and with closure afterwards. Signs that indeed show the 'Veil is thinner than we imagine'.

Ron DiFrancesco's 9/11 Story:
I had mentioned earlier about Ron DiFrancesco and that there would be more on him later. Well, it's now later.

After speaking with Brian Clarke, I was very interested in learning more about Ron DiFrancesco and what the events of 9/11 were like for him. I became even more intrigued when I received the book that Brian had suggested – *The Third Man Factor,* and began to read the first chapter where I found that Ron's story was the very first one.

My first thought was that I needed to contact Ron, and so I looked to see if he was a member of any social media group, and if he was, I'd send him a message and see if we could connect. I was successful in finding whom I thought was the right Ron, and after leaving a couple of messages Ron sent me a reply and of course he was curious as to what this might all be about. I proceeded to respond with the information as to 'why' I wanted to chat with him, and Ron cordially agree to a meeting. From there we arranged a timeframe to hold a phone conversation.

We had been trying to connect with each other for a couple of weeks, but every time we tried something had come up for one of us and we were not able to connect. Then on April 18th of 2023 I was finally able to have a phone discussion with Ron. However, during the first phone call Ron's phone died in the middle of the call. I began to think that maybe this was a Sign that perhaps we were we not meant to talk about Ron's 9/11 day's events. After all, this book is all about Signs – was this a specific Sign being sent to me? Not being exactly sure of my next steps, I waited for Ron to text me.

Later that evening Ron sent me an on-line message that he was free and to call him. We had connected once more, and when I asked him about his phone issue to my surprise Ron mentioned that he too felt like perhaps that this was a Sign that we were not supposed to chat. We both chuckled a bit at that and did go on to have a very good conversation where Ron told his story of that day's events to me.

For the most part Ron's story mirrored that of Brian's up to the time that he had left Brian when they were attempting to get Stanley out from the debris. The smoke had gotten so thick that Ron was having a very difficult time breathing (by the way though Ron was having difficulty breathing, Brian stated he had a fresh air bubble around him... another sign perhaps), and that's when Ron left Brian and went back into the stairwell. Not finding anyone there as Ron stated: "I decided to head upstairs in hopes of finding fresher air."

"I reached the 91st floor of the tower but found that there was no way to exit. I was with other colleagues and as I contemplated my next steps, I noticed that there was a lot smoke. This smoke was again making it difficult for me to breath, and as I looked around, I noticed several people were now lying on the floor as if they were asleep. Being overcome by the smoke I too was now lying down. Then as I was lying there on the floor, I heard a voice, very clearly, telling me to '**get up and get out**.'

"At that point I got up and started to make my way back down the stairwell. While heading down the stairs I was faced with more fire and smoke. Hesitating as to what to do, I again heard that voice telling me to '**keep going**.' I then pushed on down through three (3) floors of fire and debris, burning myself in the process. Further on down the stairwell I ran into three (3) firefighters coming up the stairs and they told me to keep going, that there was fresher air and less debris further down."

14

"I made it down the rest of the way, to the building entrance where I was met with others who told me that I could not go out the main doors and that I would have to go through the underground concourse. I then proceeded to the concourse level. There I ran into a colleague of mine who was having a lot of difficulty walking. We were now both making our way through the concourse when I heard what sounded like the building starting to collapse. I turned towards my colleague and said '**RUN**' and we then took off running across the concourse level and the very next thing I remember is a fire ball heading straight towards us, and then waking up three (3) days later in the hospital."

While recovering in the hospital Ron learned that he was burned over 60% of his body, that he had a head gash and he was told that his contacts had melted to his eyes. Ron has no memory of what had happened after they started running until he woke up in the hospital, no recollection of what the doctors had done to remove the contacts, and to further tend to his many wounds. Ron later learned that his colleague who was running with him, was sent to another hospital for care, and that he had died after spending six (6) weeks at that hospital.

After listening to Ron tell me his story, I asked him about his journey that day and who he thought might have been the one who had told him to get up when he was overcome by smoke and was lying down on the 91st floor, and then again told him to keep going on through the floors of fire. He told me: "all I could think of was that it was a higher power, an angel perhaps or even God."

Regardless, for me this definitely represented another presence being with Ron, and truly a 'Sign' being presented. A sign that Ron had listened to and which on that day had saved his life. That voice telling him to get up and get out and his paying attention to it and not second guessing it was what had led Ron in the right direction, ultimately saving his life.

And it was surely a Sign showing us all that the Veil is indeed thinner than we imagine.

My thoughts on 9/11 and Brian and Ron's story.

Unlike Brian, Ron had not wanted to talk much about that day, as he stated: "I know I am having survivor's guilt knowing that I lived while so many of my colleagues had perished. My constant thought of why me, why was I the lucky one to survive, permeated my mind for a long while after. However, with the passage of time and with some serious introspection, I have managed through a lot of that grief and am more comfortable talking about it today." Though as I spoke with him, I sensed the anguish of that day still very much resonating in his voice.

Both Ron's and Brian's stories, along with Stanley's (who I was unsuccessful connecting with), can be found on YouTube. Additionally, there have been several articles written about that day mentioning their stories, and the 911 commission did a full

16

detail review of that day's events and the report can be found at HTTPS://9-11commission.gov .

Let me be clear 9/11 was an act of terrorism, a cowardly sneak attack meant to do as much harm and create as much physical damage and chaos as was possible. And in its aftermath, it left a hole in the façade of the New York skyline, a hole in the hearts of those that lost loved ones and a hole in the hearts of all fellow Americans.

The paradox of 9/11 is that the horrific event was an effort meant to tear America down, to make us feel weaker, but it actually had the opposite effect. Immediately after the events of that day we all drew closer as a country and it made us stronger. We set aside our petty differences and recognized our true enemy and their desire to destroy us, but we were not going to allow that to happen.

Many died that day, with a price tag of billions set on the damage and lost productivity, and so much more dollars and time needed to rebuild. But throughout that day, and those afterwards, signs of America's strength through adversity prevailed. People began rallying, the likes of which we had not seen in quite a while. We were flying the Red, White and Blue in record numbers, country songs were written and sung in many venues, and the masses were once again attending religious services and praying for the well-being of our nation.

Todd Beamer's Flight 99 message of 'Let's Roll', and the country's message of 'We Must Never Forget' became rallying cries heard on most every radio and TV station. We were indeed witnessing the rise of America from the Twin Tower ashes.

That day of 9/11 is often referred to as one of our country's darkest days, but it was also a day that saw people helping people, people coming together regardless of who they were, regardless of race, creed, color, ethnicity – coming together as one people and one nation. Coming together as proud citizens of the United States, we were all Americans. This became one of those rare times when America truly seemed to be, as the founders intended, **'One Nation Under God'**.

Was this coming together yet another Sign being presented to us all? Were the Signs that were clearly sent to Brian and Ron, not the only ones of that day? For as a result of that day, did we not all hold our family closer? Did we not give an extra hug and kiss to our children when we tucked them into bed? Did we not renew our faith in our brothers and sisters, our community, our county and our God?

I started this book stating that I am not what you would call a Church going, Bible reading, religious type person, but I am a definite believer. I cannot deny all these many Signs that have been delivered, and for me these Signs indicate that there is more waiting for us as they say – Beyond the Veil. We should no longer question that these Signs are real and that we should be paying ever closer attention to them.

1.2 AN ADDICT, AN ANGEL AND THE REAPER

Ed Currie may not as of yet be a household name. But I'll bet that if you like spicy foods, you might have had some food enhanced by products that he produces. I interviewed Ed recently and I can tell you, he has a very interesting story to tell about his life, and especially about the SIGN that ultimately led to his survival, and the fabulous life he now leads.

Ed was born in New York City in 1963. By the age of 13, he was, in his words, **'a full blown addict'**. He had started drinking at a young age and later moved into harder drugs. By the time he reached college age, and then later into the working world, he could not go a day without getting high from alcohol and drugs.

Eventually Ed's addiction got so bad that his only goal was to score that next 'fix'. He would do anything he could to get money to buy the means feeding his addiction. Over time Ed gained a lot of weight too, eventually tipping the scales at 368 pounds. Due to the drugs and alcohol, he and his wife divorced, he lost many of his friends, and the only ones he would hear from were those that also wanted to get high.

By now it was 1999 and Ed found himself living alone in a condo, taking drugs and consuming over a gallon and a half of liquor daily. His addiction kept him motivated for more of the same, and he would oblige and do most anything necessary to ease the pain. One cold and blizzardly January day in Michigan, Ed reached rock bottom, the darkest place imaginable, all he

19

wanted to do was to stop the pain. He was suffering deep depression and debilitating feelings of despair that consumed his every thought.

With those painful emotions taking over, he began the actions he thought necessary to complete his task of stopping all of his pain and suffering. However, his plans were soon to be altered by what can only be described as an **'Angelic vision'** – and that is where his **'miracle'** begins.

Ed scurried through his condo and gathered up the alcohol and drugs which he then planned to consume in large quantities. The weather outside that January night was a full blown blizzard so he also decided to open up his front door and the windows of his condo and let the blizzard blow on in. With all the preparations made, he stripped naked, sat at the table and began drinking and taking the drugs.

Now some might argue that this next part of Ed's story just might be as a result of hallucinations from the drugs and alcohol that he consumed, but as Ed affirms, he soon had a visitor at his door. He describes this visitor as an angelic looking female who appeared and entered his condo through the opened door.

The following is excerpted from a podcast Ed did with Mike Rowe which aired on YouTube in 2023.

"There was an Angel...it was bright white and it's like radiating light...just lit up like backlighting, but forward lighting too...the angel was whiter than the light behind it".

This angelic being then spoke to Ed and told him to: **"go to Brighton Hospital"**. That is all that was said, but at the same time, as he describes it, "**all the fear, all the shame, all the guilt ... boom – went away**".

When the angelic being vanished, Ed, dumbfounded and bewildered, rose from his chair and went to the open door where he then noticed that a lot of snow had entered the condo. However, what he did not see were any footprints anywhere, just the mound of white Michigan snow that had blown in!

Thinking about what Ed was telling me I saw this 'being' as a Sign, and that sign became the catalyst that triggered the moment that Ed began his journey back to sobriety and his new life to come.

With the words of *'go to Brighton Hospital'* still ringing in his ears, Ed began to gather the necessary provisions he thought he would need for his travels to the hospital. He loaded up his car, a Camero T-Top, with, as he describes it – "*I loaded up the car with guns, alcohol and drugs, and within 20 minutes I was in my car driving to Brighton Hospital*".

Ed did not know where the hospital was but he did know where the city of Brighton was, and he figured the hospital had to be

21

somewhere near that. Ed drove in the blizzard to his friend's house in nearby Whitmore Lake, and proceeded to tell them about the angel visit and needing to go to Brighton Hospital. His friends could see that he was excitedly agitated and they attempted to calm him down, while at the same time phoning Ed's parents to let them know the situation and that they would deliver Ed to the hospital.

Upon arrival at the hospital, and again as Ed describes it – *"I knocked on the door and the person who answered said what do you want, and I said an angel sent me here"*. Immediately he was welcomed in and when he found out that Brighton Hospital was a rehab facility, he adamantly wanted to leave.

Ed was very agitated at this point. His friend Carl tried to calm him down and in doing so gave Ed a full pint of bourbon, which he immediately consumed. The hospital staff continued talking with him and after a bit longer, Ed agreed to stay and was then shown to his room where he proceeded to pass out on the bed. Five days after arriving Ed woke up finding himself being injected in the butt with phenobarbital – a known anticonvulsant drug. This had been the beginning of what would be his 33 day stay at Brighton Hospital.

The rehab facility's programs begun to show positive results in Ed's behavior. However, a wrinkle in his stay occurred when his medical insurance benefit ended, and would no longer pay for his stay and treatments. Ed was now forced to leave the facility.

Wanting to stay in the program, he found a place where he could stay that was less than two miles away from the hospital, so he could continue his treatments. However, believing that he had lost his license to drive, over the next 32 months Ed would walk to and from Brighton Hospital, attending and completing the programs necessary to bring about and maintain his sobriety.

This sobriety was something Ed had not felt in many, many years, and as an added bonus, with all that walking he did back and forth to the facility, he lost 200 pounds, now weighing 168 pounds. For the first time, in a very long time, Ed was feeling and looking great and he credits this turnaround to what he describes as a '**Miracle**'.

Ed had been a lifelong addict, scrounging to get his next fix. Worse yet, he was in a great depression and wanting to stop the all-consuming pain. But he pulls no punches when he states that *"God has relieved me of the want or need for any mood altering mind-changing substance...I have no desire to get high in any shape or form...".*

With the 33 months of rehab finished, Ed, now feeling great and looking favorably on his future, decided to pack up his belongings and move to South Carolina. There he once again began growing peppers. This was something Ed had done before, in order to get the money for the drugs and alcohol. However, this time around he would be bringing both his sobriety and the knowledge he received from studying chemistry in college with him.

Soon Ed's peppers were selling well and his life continued to flourish. He began socializing once again, making many new friends. Soon he met a woman by the name of Linda who was a devout Christian. Ed knew right away that she was special because when he told her his life story and having met an angel – as Ed tells it – *"she did not laugh"*. Not long after they were married.

Twenty four years has passed since 1999 and Ed's angelic Sign. Today he is happily married with two fabulous children and a thriving business. He told me the story of adopting his children and how that whole process came about. That was another time where he and Linda paid attention to the intervention of the Signs that had led to those adoptions. Powerful testimony and perhaps a story for another time.

Most days you can find Ed at his pepper growing farm, or operating his 'Puckerbutt' company where the peppers are turned into valuable products for sale to manufacturers and stores throughout the world. His companies employ over 130 people, and he has employed several people who, like him, were once addicts and who have managed to get themselves sober. One employee stated that: *"It kind of saved my life. I was a drug addict before and hot sauce and peppers kind of gave me a calling afterwards. Something to do with my life"*.

(https://www.youtube.com/watch?v=sKiiCQ2jhuw.   Mike Rowe –
Dirty Jobs)

Over the years Ed has experimented with breeding various
pepper varieties and created a pepper that he named the 'HP' or
Higher Power pepper. With still further experimenting Ed
developed the 'Carolina Reaper' pepper which scored him a spot
in the Guinness Book of World Records for creating the world's
hottest chili pepper with an average of 1,641,000 Scoville heat
units (SHU). For comparison purposes, a jalapeño measures
2,000 to 8,000 SHUs, while a serrano pepper is between 10,000
and 23,000 SHUs.

But 'ole Ed was not done yet. With his continued pepper
breading program, he has now come up with what he is calling
'Pepper X'. This pepper measures an average of 2.693 million
SHU's, and will soon be crowned the world's hottest, and an
added update to the Guinness Book of World Records. Also, as
Ed mentioned, there are some doctors interested in 'Pepper X'
for medicinal needs, especially in the potential treatment of
Cancer.

During my interview with Ed, he not only told me about his past,
and what he and his family are doing now, he also told me how
God has influenced his life and his belief that the event that
happened that cold Michigan night in 1999 was a turning point
for him. As he says *it's the truth and it was a miracle*. He
also said that his wife, Linda, has had her fair share of events –

what he describes as divine intervention, what I have termed Signs, and they feel very blessed by it all.

Ed's personal life revolves around his family, attending church regularly, contributing through his business to the lives and families of his employees, and giving back to his community. Through his pepper creations, Ed has also become a bit of an international celebrity and is regularly sought out by the main stream media to tell his story of how he created the hottest pepper on the planet.

One last story he told me was that after he was married, he started attending church services again. During one of the services there was communion, and his wife wanted Ed to receive communion with her. Ed told her he couldn't, not yet, and with that his wife left to walk the several rows to the front of the church to receive communion. During our interview Ed told me the reason why he could not receive communion was that he felt **'he was not yet worthy to do so'**.

While Ed sat watching, his wife proceeded to the stage where the pastor was singing and handing out communion to the parishioners, giving blessing to those that received. Ed then, with what sounded like a gulp in his voice and the fighting back of tears stated: ***"all of a sudden, the pastor stopped singing, grabbed the wine challis and the communion wafer, jumped off the stage and headed back the several rows of pews to where I was, stopping right in front of me. He then looked***

directly into my eyes, and said – you are worthy of
accepting Christ. And with that I received my communion".

Soon after that last story, our interview ended. I sat for several
minutes taking in all that Ed and I had discussed. How he went
from being a full blown addict, hitting rock bottom, in complete
despair and wanting to end the pain, to then seeing an angel,
going to Brighton Hospital, attending almost 3 years of rehab,
getting sober, turning his life around, creating the world's hottest
pepper, employing 130 people, getting married, adopting two
children and attending church services. Wow – wow – wow –
wow - wow…

This interview with Ed truly had me thinking hard about many
things, especially the Signs that present themselves in people's
lives. How that sometimes in a person's darkest hour, there can
be a light, a bright radiating light, at the end of the dark tunnel or
in this case – standing in the doorway of a condo. A light that
was observed, listened to, and which brought about a major life
change for the better. A light, or what I have termed a Sign that
brought with it a message for the receiver named Ed Currie.

Some Signs might redirect your thoughts, while other signs might
redirect your day, and still other signs might redirect your life – as
it did for Ed. Whatever the Sign's intention or meaning, in this
author's opinion, definitely shows that the Veil is Thinner than we
Imagine!

1.3 A Deadly Flight, a Phone Call, and a Safe Landing

On Good Friday, April 7, 2023 a movie called '*On a Wing and a Prayer*' was released for the first time making its debut on Amazon Prime. This movie is based upon the real life events that presented themselves to Doug White and his family while flying in a King Air airplane (call letters N559DW) heading back home to Louisiana after having attended his brother's funeral held on Marco Island in Florida.

Shortly after takeoff, about ten (10) minutes into the flight, the pilot – 67 year old Joe Cabuk suffers sudden cardiac arrest and dies. According to Doug White, Joe's death was quick, sudden and final. This now left Doug, who had been seated next to Joe, alone in the cockpit. Doug's family, his wife Terry and their two daughters were sitting behind him in the passenger cabin.

Doug knew he needed to act, and he needed to act fast, while at the same time somehow managing to keep his emotions in check. His immediate need was for safely landing the plane and saving his family. Doug quickly grabbed the radio microphone, and contacting the control tower he stated **"I've got to declare an emergency. My pilot's deceased. I need help". "I need to get this on the ground. I'm flyin' a King Air"**.

The first contact Doug made was with Lisa Grimm out of the Miami Control Center. Doug told her that the King Air was on auto-pilot and the plane was climbing. Lisa – accessing the situation, had Doug dis-engage the auto-pilot in order to stop the ascent and level off the plane. Turning off the auto-pilot left the plane at an altitude of 18,000 feet and Doug now had to manually fly the plane, and hopefully, with the help from the control tower personal, bring the plane down for a safe landing.

Doug remembers saying to **Lisa "You find me the longest, widest runway you can, ma'am"**. Lisa, consulting with her team, figured that it was best to send him to Ft. Myers airport as they had a long and wide runway there, some 12,000 feet long, giving Doug the maximum amount of runway to land the plane. Lisa also ordered that airspace be cleared of all traffic and the traffic controllers proceeded to aid the other pilots routing them away from the path that the King Air plane was heading.

Lisa then handed Doug over to the controllers at the Ft Myers airport. The only issue was that Ft Myers on-duty personnel did not have flying experience, except for one individual, Brian Norton, who had just clocked out for the day and was currently on the way to his car to head home. One of the people from the control tower immediately ran outside to try and stop Brian from leaving and to alert him of the emergency.

Brian was successfully stopped and brought to the TRACON center (more on that later) and not the control tower. Once there he was seated at the radar monitor alongside Dan Favio, who at the time was a Developmental Controller. Brian immediately contacted Doug to introduce himself and get apprised of Doug's current altitude, wind speed and other pertinent information. Brian also let Doug know that he would be with him until he landed safely on the ground.

Though Brian did have some flight experience, unfortunately it was not in a King Air. Discussing their alternatives for safely landing the plane, Dan mentioned that his buddy Kari Sorenson, who as Dan describes him – **"he's the smartest person I know"** knew a lot about aircraft including the King Air. Unfortunately, Kari lived in Danbury Connecticut some 1200 miles due north. However, believing that this was their best hope, Dan, avoiding protocol, used his own cell phone to call his buddy Kari and advise him of the situation with Doug White's plane.

Kari and his fiancé Ashley Harrison had been home working on Kari's antique Model A car, and were about to go to their friend's house for an Easter dinner, when Kari received Dan's call on his cell. Kari's greeting of **"hey buddy what's up"** was immediately met by Dan's interruption, with his explanation of the situation with Doug White and his family.

> *For background on Kari, he owns Tally-Ho Aviation, LLC in Danbury Connecticut (www.tally-hoav.com). Kari's services include, but not limited to: General Aviation Maintenance, Dynamic Propeller Balancing, Ferry Services, Electronics International (EI) Dealer, Diamond Aircraft Factory Trained and Certified, Aerobatic Aircraft Maintenance, Light Sport Aircraft Maintenance, Fabric Covering and Repair, Airframe Repair, Engine Overhaul and more.*

Kari immediately jumped into action asking about the pilots' flight history and the plane's speed and pitch. Kari also received the plane's tail number and Ashley immediately began using their computer to look up the plane's specific information. Additionally, Kari asked Ashley to get any books and papers that he might have had regarding the King Air airplane. Ashley quickly returned with the needed books and a poster size layout of the schematic of the plane's dashboard layout.

Kari, analyzing all of the information he was receiving, knew immediately that the best chance they all had of landing safely and saving everyone's lives was to somehow teach Doug how to fly that plane, and he had maybe 20 minutes for the lesson. Kari then took the cockpit layout, and his phone, went to his living room and settled into his easy chair with the cockpit layout in front of him. He had now set himself up as if he was actually inside of the plane's cockpit sitting in front of the controls – thereby seeing exactly what Doug would be seeing.

The King Air was a twin engine plane and much more powerful, and with more instrumentation than Doug would have been accustomed to in the Cessna plane that Doug had learned to fly many years prior. Doug had stated that the cockpit looked like the inside of the space shuttle to him with all of the instrumentation, dials, gauges and such. (And as he stated in a later interview: "You just focus your fear and go into a zone." "There's no time to chit-chat, or lock up. Just 'git er done.")

Kari needed to get Doug use to flying the plane and he told Doug to forget about all of those other dials and to focus on the 6-pack. The 6-pack is a group of gauges labeled as such because the 6 gauges are ordered in a way that resemble the 'looking at the bottoms of a 6-pack of cans. Kari needed to teach Doug how to fly this plane, though what he really wanted was to have Doug back on the auto-pilot, but Doug did not know how to change the current heading that the deceased pilot had previously set for the auto-pilot.

Kari had been briefed that Doug had some single engine flight experience. Several years earlier Doug had learned to fly, and over the last six (6) months Doug had completed 25-30 hours flight time in a Cessna 172. Knowing this and quickly thinking out of the box, Kari then instructed Doug that he should fly the plane as if it was a single engine plane,

Brian and Dan who are on the ground at Ft. Myers airport, are in what is called TRACON (Terminal Radar Approach Control), which is an area beneath the control tower that has no windows, but does have radar screens with which to track the airplanes' movements. This is essentially what might be considered the basement area of the Control Tower. What this means is that no one who had direct communication with Doug that day, actually saw the plane while in flight or during landing.

It is also important to know that Kari never spoke directly to Doug. Instead, it was a series of relayed messages, like when you were in school and the first kid in the row of desks turns to the next kid and relays a message (the old Telephone game). This then continues until all of the kids have received the message and then the last one to receive it tells the class what the message was that they had received. Dan was on the phone with Kari (in Danbury) and when Dan received Kari's instructions for Doug, Dan then told Brian who then relayed the message to Doug, to which Doug's reply was then given to Brian who relayed it to Dan who then relayed it to Kari.

Kari knew that Doug had one shot at landing the plane. Kari also knew that the odds of all of the needed steps happening correctly and the plane landing safely was probably around 10 percent. But Kari, who had lost both his father and stepfather in airplane accidents, knew he had to get Doug and his family down safely and he was committed to doing so.

Dan kept Kari updated on Doug's progress and Kari kept feeding Dan with a series of altitudes and headings. All of them worked together, as if they were synchronized rhythmically to relay the data back and forth. As Dan fed Kari the data, Kari sitting in front of the cockpit diagram would then figure out the next set of instructions to feed back to Doug.

Kari began feeding instructions that would enable Doug to head towards the Ft. Myers airport and its runways. Kari sends instruction for Doug to begin using the plane's flaps in order to slow the plane down, while at the same time Brian is also vectoring Doug towards his final approach. Kari also instructs that the landing gear be engaged. Dan tells Brian who then tells Doug who complies and in doing so he hears the Master Caution Warning alarm. Kari is then provided that information, to which he instructs that Dan should ignore it and just continue to fly the plane.

Doug, who has managed to block out the cockpit warning alarms as well as his emotions, is doing a great job flying and has brought the plane down to 3000 feet. Kari then advises that the flaps must now be down all the way. With the message relayed to Doug, Kari is informed that the flaps are now down and Doug's plane is stabilized and heading straight towards the runway. Kari asks if Doug knows where the brakes are and after the message relay, Doug confirms that he does.

34

Soon the countdown starts – 3000, 2000, 1000 feet... then 500
feet, 400, 300, 200, 100 and Doug has now landed the plane
safely, no skidding and only used 3500 feet of the runway. Doug
radios to find out what taxiway from the runway he should take,
and after doing so, he brings the plane to a complete stop.

Many of the emergency folks began to approach the plane and
Doug was then given the **'kill the engine'** sign (hand across the
throat) by the EMT's who were now in front of the plane.   The
problem was that Doug had no idea how to turn off the King Air
engines.

The Ft. Myers airport had been shut down to all traffic and there
were several airliners waiting to be released for takeoff. One of
the waiting pilots who had overheard the conversation between
Doug and ground control, interjects and mentioned that he had a
good bit of King Air experience and he would be willing to talk to
Doug and help him through the procedure for shutting off the
engines. Ground control granted him permission and an
unknown airline pilot walked Doug through the steps of turning
off the engines.

With the engines successfully shut off, Doug and his family
gathered their belongings and left the plane. Once safely on the
ground the whole event finally hit Doug, and what had been his
calm demeanor came to an end as his emotions of the ordeal
began to surface and take ahold of him.

Dan immediately informs Kari that Doug's plane is down, but without being able to see it from the TRACON facility, Dan had no idea of how the landing went and what shape the plane and its passengers were in. Dan tells Kari that he will go out and check and would call him back. It is then that the next strange event happened.

When Dan saw that the plane had landed safely and that the people were fine, that the plane didn't even have a scratch on it, nor even a scuffed tire from the landing; it was then that Dan went to call Kari to let him know that everything was fine and that he'd call him back later with more details. However, that is when Dan's phone immediately went dead and I don't mean that it was out of battery and needed to be charged, I mean the phone was dead and no longer working.

Kari, in Danbury, was left for a few days wondering what all had happened with the landing and the White family. Kari tried repeatedly calling Dan, but all he could do was to leave a message. Kari states that he is a bit panicked and that he had been pacing his living room floor. Three days later, after Dan had purchased a new phone, he then was able to call Kari and relate the rest of this miraculous story.

Having the conversations with Doug, and with Kari and Ashley, I asked if they felt that there were Signs or perhaps even another presence with them that day. A Sign or a presence that was a guiding influence enabling them to work together to get the plane landed safely. Doug, as a Christian, stated that he knew that the angels were with him and his family throughout the flight, as he told me that **"people of faith – walking in the light, you have God with you 24/7 and with that you have His servant Angels who were already there with me and my family"**. Doug also stated that he had what he called a focused fear, an almost inner peace, and he knew that God was in control.

As Kari, Ashley and Doug stated to me that by having all the needed parts and procedural steps coming together as they did that day – that in doing so they believed that the successful landing of the plane was nothing short of a miracle. During the phone calls with Doug and the one with Kari and Ashley they each proceeded to list off the various parts and steps, and did so in a very similar manner.

For example,

- Dan knowing Kari, and Dan being in the TRACON facility that day observing as part of his training.
- Kari being home to receive Dan's call, as he and Ashley had not yet left for their Easter dinner with friends.
- Kari having the cockpit layout schematic for the King Air.
- Kari and Ashley working together to get the needed information and to set Kari up with the cockpit schematic – as if Kari was actually in the plane's cockpit seat.
- Doug flying out over the gulf through many clouds, only to find no clouds on his return just minutes later.

- No wind in Ft Myers at the airport, in the spring time, near the gulf, as Doug lands, and as he stated – **"when does that ever happen"**.
- Brian Norton, who had flight experience – just not in a King Air, was leaving for the day – but who was caught just before he had left the parking lot and brought back inside to handle the landing.
- Brian viewing the radar screen and noticing that all air traffic was cleared and the only target on the screen was that of the King Air plane.
- Lisa Grimm who also had flight experience and knew how to keep Doug flying until he was handed safely off to Ft Myers for the landing.
- The calmness of the communications chain, and especially Brian's reassuring calm voice.
- Dan's phone surviving just long enough for the plane to successfully land and then mysteriously dying – to the point that Dan needed to buy a new phone.
- The King Air plane being able to go to Ft Myers airport where they had a big 'ol runway that, as they say, was wide enough and long enough to handle space shuttle landings.

Doug, Kari and Ashley, all told me that everyone was where they needed to be that day and with the tools and knowledge necessary to assist Doug on the safe landing of the plane. This was not just happenstance, this was guidance, and as Doug stated **"this was as it was meant to be"**. Kari told me that if any one of the items listed above was not to happen, and in the order that it had to happen, then the whole landing would not have been successful, and most likely all passengers would have died. Kari knew that they had one attempt at landing the plane and that there would be no second chances.

I began this by talking about the movie *On a Wing and a Prayer*. During my conversations I learned a few things about the making of the movie. For example, the movie was first pitched to MGM networks years earlier and it had been turned down. Then, five (5) years later it was brought back around for a second time, landing on the desk of the people in charge of the spiritual programming for MGM, and where this time it was approved. The movie came out fourteen (14) years after the incident, where it was brought out on Good Friday with a spiritual message.

Doug told me that he has heard from countless people, via social media, that this movie has caused them to return to religious services, to reconcile with family members, to make amends for past wrongs, and in the case of Dan Favio – well you saw in the movie that he appeared to have a drinking problem. In actuality he did and the events of that day and how it all unfolded has caused him to now turn away from alcohol.

Doug also told me that he believed the movie came out exactly when it was supposed to. He is among those that recognize that there is a Christian (religious) revival happening in this country and this movie is helping to spread the word. And in Dan's case

39

specifically, he was baptized about a year and a half (1.5 years) after the event happened.

I find myself agreeing with Doug's comment – especially remembering what I had read about the revival event at Ashbury College in Wilmore Kentucky. The event had started on February 8th of this year (2023) and was brought to an end on February 23, some 15 days later. The school decided to end the on-campus services after tens of thousands of visitors, from around the world, flooded the campus and the small town of Wilmore, Kentucky, overwhelming locals and blocking traffic. As I stated to Doug – it's like a ripple in the lake. The ripple starts off small, but grows and grows to the point that it reaches all shores. We agreed that this particular ripple, being the revival of Christianity, is still in its growth stage.

Another thing I was to learn while talking with Kari and Ashley is that this incident is now being used as a learning exercise in both the Pilot Flight Training classes, and in the Air Traffic Controller training classes. The action steps taken that day had represented **'out of the box'** thinking in a crisis situation and provided a very valuable message and teaching exercise.

Reviewing all of this, and thinking if there is some deeper meaning here – for me it's a message of faith. The understanding that steps had to happen in the correct order to land the plane – no second chances. Understanding that people needed to be positioned on that day, in the right places at the right time and if one of them were absent or different, then there

40

might just have been an entirely different outcome. The fact that Brian and Dan were in TRACON and that Dan knew Kari and Ashley and they had the needed information about the King Air plane, and knew exactly how to help. The understanding that there were clouds and wind when Doug was flying off into the gulf, but then mere moments later on his turn back towards Ft. Myers airport – the skies were clear blue with no wind. One needn't ask how this happens.

Faith – what else need be said – but perhaps that maybe the Veil is thinner than we imagine.

"My mama always told me that miracles happen every day. Some people don't think so, but they do." - Forest Gump

1.4 BASKETBALL, DREAMS AND HOPE!

"But our country was captivated by your amazing story on the basketball court. I think it's a story of Coach Johnson's willingness to give a person a chance. It's a story of Dave and Debbie's deep love for their son, and it's a story of a young man who found his touch on the basketball court, which in turn, touched the hearts of citizens all across the country."

President George W. Bush

President Bush: "I am very honored to meet you Jason, can I call you J-Mac?"

J-Mac: "Yes, sir."

President Bush: "You can call me George W."

That was the intro on the Rochester NY tarmac March 14, 2006, as President George W. Bush met Jason McElwain. Known simply as J-Mac – the autistic student from Greece Athena High School – Greece NY, was the student-coach manager of the Greece Athena Trojans Basketball Team.

J-Mac was born autistic and he would not speak until he was five (5) years old. Growing up, J-Mac's dream was to be like all the other kids, to run and play, and to be a typical kid. Once he began talking, his older brother Josh started taking him everywhere. Some of those outings would be to the basketball courts, and that is where J-Mac began his passion for the game, and some might say that is where he had found his purpose.

J-Mac became obsessed with basketball, reading and learning about the game, and when he could, with weather permitting, he would shoot baskets from sun-up until he was forced to come in for the day. When he got to junior high, he wanted to try out for the basketball team, which he did, but unfortunately, he didn't make the cut. However due to his determination, and with a little prodding to the school, made by his mom Debbie, a student-manager position was created for Jason, one that he embraced by being at every practice and showing up on game nights in white shirt and tie. This then became J-Mac's passion throughout his high school career, showing up for all the off season practices too.

42

With his senior year upon him, and the basketball season beginning, J-Mac was once again back as the student manager of the team. However, as this year's season began the team's coach, Jim Johnson, had a surprise planned for J-Mac. J-Mac was told by Coach Johnson, that his gift to J-Mac for all of his hard work with the team over the years, is that "**I want you to suit up for Senior Night game (February 15, 2006) and sit on the bench with your teammates**". This had been a dream of J-Mac's for many years. Coach Johnson also stated that **"I can't promise you'll get to play",** and J-Mac acknowledged that he understood.

The team immediately started off with two wins, but then went on a losing streak as some internal strife began infecting the team's morale. The next practice for the team saw the coach setting them all down and saying that he did not have all the answers and wanted to hear from the players as to how they could right the ship.

For a while it was quiet, but then one player speaks up and makes a suggestion, then soon another player and eventually several players speak with their suggestions. Coach Johnson was enthusiastically taking in all of the players suggestions, and as a result of that day's team talk, subsequent changes were made that began the start of the team coming together, and with this renewed morale they were back on a winning streak.

Senior night was now happening and the word soon spread throughout the school that J-Mac would be suiting up. For this particular game, the bleachers were packed with students holding up placards with Jason's face on it. Often, throughout the game, they could be heard shouting and chanting J-Mac's name.

The Greece Athena Trojans were having a good game and soon saw themselves realizing a very comfortable lead over their opponents. And with just four (4) minutes to go and given their lead in the game – Coach Johnson looked down the bench and pointed to J-Mac who immediately jumped up eager to go onto the court, almost forgetting to first check in. Excitedly this five-foot-six – one hundred (100) pound petite autistic kid, with his big dream about to be realized, checked in and officially made his way out onto the court for his first ever appearance in a game.

J-Mac was obviously nervous and it took a bit for him to settle into the flow. Soon his teammates passed him the ball and when he launched it for his first shot – it was an air-ball, at least six (6) feet off the mark. J-Mac's second (2nd) attempt was not much better, but then on his third (3rd) shot from the 3-point position on the court he swishes it. The folks in the bleachers erupted in cheer and wildly waved their J-Mac-faced placards – it was pure delight for J-Mac and total excitement for his teammates and the spectators (cue the angelic music).

J-Mac's dream was about to get even bigger, as he was not done by a long shot (pun intended). His teammates, without any thought or regard for themselves, and without any encouragement from the coaches, on each trip down the court, continued to find J-Mac and feed him the ball. Time and time again, his teammates looking for J-Mac and passing him the ball, and J-Mac then finishing the job. Again, and again he kept scoring, 3-pointer after 3-pointer – six (6) of them in total. As J-Mac stated afterwards – **"I was hot as a pistol"**.

With game time running out, the ball was passed to J-Mac one last time, and as he dribbled down the court, and with him now positioned a few feet behind the 3 point line with mere seconds remaining, ball in hand, he sends it up, what is typically termed an NBA 3 pointer, swish and with that he scored his final 3-pointer of his 'Story Book' night.

With the sounding of the horn signaling the end of the game, pandemonium broke out from the bleachers, the crowd spilling onto the gym floor. The teammates and the spectators mobbed J-Mac throwing him on their shoulders and as he would later say – **"it was like we had won the championship game"**.

With the end of the game, and after his four (4) minutes of play time, J-Mac had totaled a remarkable twenty (20) points and was the team high scorer for the night, and what a storied night it was. The dream J-Mac had since he was a youngster running and playing with his older brother, a dream that one day he would be just like all the other kids, out on the court, ball in hand, playing the game of his life, had just been realized.

For those who have watched the movie *Rudy*, with actor Sean Astin playing the part of Rudy Ruettiger, this particular Senior Night's basketball game indeed had that Rudy-esk feeling. Rudy was a walk-on player with hopes and dreams of playing for the University of Notre Dame Fighting Irish football team. Rudy, like J-Mac, put in the work and effort and had the heart, but due to his size, at best he was relegated to the practice squad. However, on the last game of the season, with mere seconds left in the game, and Notre Dame ahead in scoring, Rudy was given his chance to play. And through this game, J-Mac too had realized his Rudy moment.

But that was not the end of J-Mac's remarkable journey – as the media caught attention of this story and J-Mac's magnificent accomplishment – he, along with Coach Johnson, were in great demand for talk shows, newspaper articles, TV news programs and the like. And to top it all off, as I had started this story, President George W. Bush flew into Rochester personally to meet and shake the hand of this young man called J-Mac.

Still, the stardom was not over for J-Mac, as he was also nominated that year for an ESPY award. And on the night of the award ceremony Jason's name was called as the winner of the ESPY for 'Best Moment in Sports', having beat out the likes of Kobe Bryant (who J-Mac idolized) and his 81 point game, along with two other fabulous athletes. There he stood, at the podium having not spoken a word until he was five years old, this somewhat shy nervous autistic kid with a big dream, giving his acceptance speech that his brother had written for him, in front of hundreds in the audience, and as he says – **"the whole world is watching"**. And then at the end, his words spoken loud and clear, with graciousness and gratitude – **"Thank you God"**.

Having spoken recently with Coach Johnson, I asked him if he had thought about that night and why he felt it was the right thing to put Jason into the game. Coach responded that he had already played the other seniors, that the team had a very comfortable lead, and that it was the right time to do so. However, when J-Mac missed that first shot, the coach stated that he was sitting on the sidelines, head in hands, asking **"Dear God just let him get a basket"**.

Well God heard and answered, and with that J-Mac proceeded to score several baskets for a total of 20 points, and did it in the 4 minutes remaining in the game – outscoring all of his other teammates. Coach Johnson stated later that after J-Mac's performance he thought God had to be a basketball fan. J-Mac's dad David commented afterwards in an interview **"that the planets were in alignment that night, I don't know how else to say it"**. And as J-Mac would say in a later interview **"I've never shot that well in my life"**.

One thing I learned much later while listening to a podcast of Coach Johnson's, was that while J-Mac was playing and hitting his shots, and with one minute to go, the coach felt a tap on his shoulder. When he turned to see who it was, he found Jason's mother there and she, with tears in her eyes, told the coach that

47

this was the best gift he could have given her son. Needless to say, both of them now had tears in their eyes.

Afterwards, J-Mac along with Coach Johnson were kept very busy fielding calls from TV and radio personalities wanting them to appear on their shows. Later Coach Johnson would write a book called **A Coach and a Miracle** portraying that night's events. Movie producers were calling, and even though the rights were bought to the story, the movie has not yet been released.

As for J-Mac he wasn't done with sports and he soon set his sights on the Boston Marathon. He trained hard for it, and in 2014 he finished with a sub 3-hour time. He also went onto write his own book titled **The Game of My Life**.

J-Mac was that typical high school teenager, head full of dreams of playing basketball for his school team and on that night his dream was realized. Wondering about how Jason's mom and dad must have felt about the game, and then meeting the president, and the other media celebrities, I can only imagine the pride of the night that they saw their son scoring shot after shot, then being hoisted onto his teammate's shoulders. And to top it off, to see him standing at the podium of the ESPY awards and reading his prepared speech. The hope that they had for their son all those many years, I'm sure gave them renewed vigor that J-Mac's future would be one for the books!

Towards the end of the interview, I asked the coach if he was aware that he had started something that has now been repeated several times in high schools all across the country and not just for basketball. Kids with disabilities, on multiple occasions, have been given opportunities to become a one-time player for a game in football, basketball, wrestling and soccer, thereby realizing their own dreams. As Coach Johnson then stated – **"perhaps this is God's way of giving hope"**.

The video and its story have now become a Sign that has given hope to so many others. And from the repeat of this story and seeing so many schools' sports coach's embracing this and allowing a player with a disability to realize their dream and have their spotlight play time, I truly think that the Sign is doing exactly what it was meant to do. The message that just because your child might have some disability should not hold them back, but instead this Sign gives them hope that they too can achieve their dreams.

"One person can change the world by giving people Hope". This was part of the closing remarks of a speech given by US Navy Admiral William H. McRaven, at the University-Wide Commencement – University of Texas at Austin, May 17, 2014. McRaven is a former Navy Seal Officer and is a retired United States Navy four-star admiral.

Thinking about this story and what it has meant for Jason and his family, and to countless others with disabilities who have seen J-Mac's Senior Night video, as Coach Johnson has correctly

49

stated, it has brought hope to many. By the way, from a search on YouTube for a video of J-Mac's storied game, and quickly seeing the first five (5) different YouTube search result postings, and there are many more, the video of that special night has garnered well over four (4) million views!

The video of this game has made international headlines, from the *BBC News and Daily Telegraph* in the United Kingdom, to *The Age* in Australia, and to the *Scoop* in New Zealand (**https://en.wikipedia.org/wiki/Jason_McElwain**). After seventeen (17) years, as of the writing of this book, the video is still being viewed and the books are still selling.

They say that God does work in mysterious ways. He also has a fondness for what some might have thought of as the underdog. And let us never forget how the other saying goes – that the meek shall inherit the Earth. As for me, the power of this Sign speaks volumes as the story of J-Mac and the night he defied the stereotype of kids with his disability, achieving his dream, will continue to give hope to many others for years to come!

"Never Give Up, Never Give In" – J-Mac

Coach Johnson gave a kid a chance, a chance to realize his dream which seemed simple enough, but who knew what this act of generosity would mean and how the ongoing story would develop. Coach Johnson was not having a great year that year, by his own admission, as there was some disruption being expressed from some parents, and that was filtering to the team players. However, he had viewed J-Mac as a uniter on the team, and he played to Jason's strength all year which had a positive team impact, and as an award to Jason, he allowed him to play in his first and only game on Senior Night in front of hundreds in attendance. And as you can see from the telling of his story, J-Mac did not disappoint.

During my interview with Coach Johnson, I learned a bit about the coach's dream too. The coach told me that he had his own dreams of winning a sectional title and after many years of coaching he still had not realized that dream. He also told me that he was always a bit uptight during game nights and even during some practices. Even though he wanted only to draw out the best from his players, he knew that sometimes there might have been some resentment to his coaching style and actions.

Truth be told I knew this about the coach as my own son played varsity basketball at Greece Athena, having been both co-team captain and awarded MVP status during his senior year. My son would tell me a bit about the coach and some of the days, as he would say, **"The coach was definitely a bit rough today"**. The coach mentioned during the interview that he just could not relax when he was coaching, and that he knew he had to settle back a bit and let the game play out, but there was that drive in him that would rise up and just interfere.

Well that all changed on that night, as there was a second dream soon to be realized. After that game, the coach told me, he felt a calmness come over him. He couldn't explain it, but he said it was a feeling that he had not had before. And with this new calmness, plus a team riding high with renewed vigor, the Greece Athena Trojans went on to win sectionals that year.

Coach Jim Johnson's dream had also been realized, yet another Sign that something tremendous had happened that night not just for J-Mac, but for the coach too. And to top it off – during the remainder of the coach's career the Greece Athena Trojans basketball team went onto to win even more sectional titles for a grand total of six (6) titles under the coach's leadership.

Inspirational, a miracle, gratefulness, and gives hope, are all words that have been used to describe what the passionate act of Coach Jim Johnson meant to J-Mac, his family, and to countless others who were there that night. And it has continued on to those who have seen the replay of that awe inspiring moment when a coach pointed to a player with autism, and gave him his time in the spotlight.

For a video of the game that J-Mac played go to: ESPN J-Mac Video - YouTube (https://www.youtube.com/watch?v=O-nMab6XDNI)

And J-Mac's story has continued to give hope to others. The following video highlights just two of the many stories that show how J-Mac's story has continued to have an impact. The Jason McElwain story inspires others (All it takes is one shot) - YouTube .(https://www.youtube.com/watch?v=fLeggFILXuU)

52

You have heard the expression that God works in mysterious ways. Well, that is not actually stated in the bible. The phrase is from a hymn by William Cowper in 1773. The closest bible reference maybe from Ecclesiastes 11:5, "God's ways are as mysterious as the pathway of the wind and as the manner in which a human spirit is infused into the little body of a baby while it is yet in its mother's womb".

The Signs that were present that night, as the coach and others have stated, have truly made a difference through the spreading of Hope. Signs that the Veil really is thinner than we imagine.

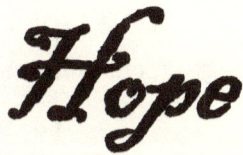

1.5 MY WIFE, HER DAD, AND OUR SNOWY TRIP

Sharon's dad Jim liked spending time outdoors and often went camping, pulling a camper with his pick-up and visiting many of the country's national parks. When he retired, her dad did a lot more of this activity and truly enjoyed the time on the road with his wife and their dog(s).

He definitely enjoyed the travel but before long the years began to catch up with him, and on one eventful day as he was doing some work using a ladder, Jim mis-stepped off the ladder, falling and breaking his hip. Soon after recovering from the broken hip, he fell again, this time hitting his head.

This was the second of recent falls he had and this one was going to be his last as Jim wound up in the hospital. He suffered a severe concussion and what was described as a brain fluid leak. This resulted in his need of constant care. Eventually he was moved to an adult care facility.

Jim had many visitors while in the residency, and we were told that this was probably going to be his last residency before he would succumb to his condition and be called home to his final resting. Upon receiving this news, Sharon wanted to pay her father what could be 'one last visit'. A visit that would be both one of joy and sadness given the situation.

Sharon and I made the arrangements and loaded up the car. We made sure to grab some provisions for the long drive and letting the kids know of our plans, we then headed out on our way. The day before we left, I had received my new floor mats for the car, and boy would we need them on this trip as there was really bad winter weather forecasted between Rochester NY and Chicago Illinois, a trip that would normally take about 12 hours was going to be extended for sure. However, given the circumstances with her dad we had little choice, especially if the worst was to happen to him and we miss our last chance of seeing him alive.

It was mid-afternoon when we departed home and over the next few hours of driving on the New York State Thruway, the roads remained fairly snow free. We were able to make some good time, though soon we entered Pennsylvania, where things took a turn for the worst as the hilly terrain and higher elevation there, led to some difficult driving with near white-out conditions.

We kept driving and the more we drove the darker it got as the sun was setting, and the worse it got with the snow and road conditions. As the driver, I wanted to make sure to keep us safe, but I also wanted to see that Sharon would have some time with her father in his last days.

We drove on a bit further, but both Sharon and I recall hearing that inner voice saying, it's time to pull over for the night. I can't speak for Sharon, but I did ignore the voice for a while as I wanted to get Sharon to Chicago as quick as I could. After all I spent several years driving in Minnesota winters so I thought I was capable of handling this. However, the more we proceeded it was becoming abundantly clear to us both that we were somehow being persuaded to pull off the road, an almost unbearable insistence to not proceed any further. We finally succumb to this nagging sense to exit the road and we did so at the very next exit. Finding a hotel with a vacancy we booked the room for the night, parked the car, and gathering our necessities, we then settled into our room for the evening.

Very early the next morning we went to the lobby to grab some breakfast and inquired at the front desk about the condition of the road ahead. We were informed that all was now fine as they had cleared the accident from last evening and reopened the road. We asked about what had happened and were informed that around 10pm a few miles down the road, a tractor trailer had lost control, jack knifed and spun into some cars and then into the median. This accident blocked all oncoming (westbound) traffic, essentially closing down the road. The reason that the time is important is that it was around 9:45pm when we felt that overwhelming prompting to stop for the evening. Had we stayed on the road we would have been directly in the area of that accident and may have even been involved in it.

Receiving this news sent shivers down my spine and to think that we could have been involved in the accident and that the worse possible scenario could have happened, was not the thoughts I wanted to be having – but indeed I was.

Knowing that the road was now open and drivable, we quickly grabbed our belongings, filled our travel mugs with coffee and continued our drive to Chicago. When we drove down the highway, we passed the tractor trailer which was partially on its

56

side in the median with a good portion of the trailer missing. We certainly felt ourselves lucky, counting our blessings as we passed through the accident portion of the road.

The weather cooperated and the rest of the drive was uneventful. Early that afternoon we reached the facility where Sharon's father was, in plenty of time to spend a good several hours with him.

During the visit we could see that Jim was not doing well and that his health was deteriorating. Though Jim was not able to speak much, Sharon was able to spend some quality time with him, and the two of them even managed to sing a song together, a song that Sharon remembered her dad singing to her when she was a little girl, that Sharon had also sung to our children when they were little. That song was called '**Little Sir-Echo'**, and though Jim was not able to say a lot – he did do a pretty good job of singing the song, remembering the words, singing slowly as his physical capability had allowed.

We spent as much time with Jim as we could, knowing that this would most likely be the last time we would see him alive, which as it turned out was true. Saying our good-byes, we headed to a local hotel for the evening and grabbed some dinner. Afterwards we prepped as much as we could for the drive home the next day, and then headed to bed.

The drive home was uneventful with mostly just light hearted chatter in the car; Sharon reminiscing about growing up and the time spent with her dad. There were also times of silence as I knew Sharon was doing a lot of thinking about life, about her dad, about family in general.

About a month after our visit, we received the news that Jim had passed. The news, though expected, was still unsettling, especially for Sharon. This was the first of her parents to pass, and though we both had experienced death in our families, it had been several decades earlier and this was happening now.

This death brought thoughts of our own immortality and the need to count our blessings every day, to be thankful, and above all else to keep our family even closer than before.

I have thought back on that time, the driving, the bad snowstorm, the overwhelming need to pull off the road and not continue on. Why did we choose that exit and not try for one more up the road? Why did we both feel compelled, as if it was an urgency, to get off the road at that time?   Was that us using our common sense, or was it us being directed and guided by forces beyond - keeping us safe? A Sign that perhaps indeed the Veil is thinner than we imagine.

"Often it is just as well that we do not know the danger we escaped when we rush in where Angel's fear to tread."
Carl Jung

2 GROUPING TWO: END OF LIFE AND VISITATION DREAMS

Have you had dreams of a departed loved one that were so vivid and so lifelike, dreams where days and even months later you can recall every detail?

Within this section will be stories that highlight both Visions and Dreams that not only accompany a person's end of life experience, but also those of the bereaved. These types of signs will often have meaning only for the recipient(s), but can at times apply to a broader audience. Many of these dreams will often leave the recipient feeling an overwhelming sense of comfort and at other times feeling a sense of relief.

Shared with permission by Mrs. Frollien

2.1 END OF LIFE DREAMS, DR. KERR, AND OUR MOM'S

Another form of visitation dreams, called End-of-life-experiences (ELE's) dreams, have been reported by the dying and their relatives for centuries. These dreams have permeated throughout folk cultures as rumors and tall tales.

Still today, stories from Japan, United States, India, China and many other countries all having reports of the near-death dreams and visions that the soon to be departed have experienced. A study among relatives in India showed that 30 per cent of their dying relatives reported having such ELE type experiences.

One person who has delved deeply into pre-death ELE type dreams is Dr. Christopher Kerr from Hospice & Palliative Care of Buffalo NY (https://www.drchristopherkerr.com). Hospice is a service for people whose death is imminent, and the goal of the health personnel who work there is not to save lives, instead they are there to soothe, support and comfort the patients until their life end.

Dr. Kerr, as a young cardiologist, applied for a weekend job at Hospice Buffalo NY. His mission was to help the patient fight death through his skill and modern-day medicine. "Like many physicians, I'd never considered that there might be more to death than an enemy to be fought", Dr. Kerr writes in his book *Death Is But a Dream*, published in 2020.

Dr. Kerr was curious about dreams and visions his patients were having before their death. One of Dr. Kerr's patients was a 72-year-old woman. One day the young doctor was present while the family was spending time with the ill woman. And as Dr. Kerr observed the dying woman began to rock an invisible baby in her arms. She kissed and stroked the infant, whom she called Danny, and seemed extremely peaceful and full of happiness.

The relatives didn't understand what was happening. Was this a hallucination or perhaps reaction to medication, as no one knew of any child named Danny, until the dying woman's sister arrived the next day and the mystery was solved. She was able to relate that this was the name of a stillborn child that the ill woman had prior to her other children being born. As the sister recalls, the dying woman had been very distressed by this incident, but had never told her family about it.

For Dr. Kerr, it soon became clear that the incident was not unique at all. The staff at the hospice shared that many of their patients had special dreams and visions in the time before their death, and over time Dr. Kerr met a number of dying people who had these experiences. His interest was piqued and soon he began in earnest to study and research this phenomenon.

The above information was from an article in **Sciencenorway.no** by journalist Ingrid Spilde. The information was paraphrased and condensed, but the message is clear that there is an interesting phenomenon that has occurred with people who are at death's door, perhaps peeking through it – something that I have seen termed being in or at **'Thin Places'**. The Thin Place is a place where the Veil between this world and the eternal world is thin, where one is said to be able to walk in two worlds – that is, the worlds are fused together, where the two worlds then become one.

"There is an indefinable, mysterious power that pervades everything. I feel it, though I do not see it. It is this unseen power that makes itself felt and yet defies all proof, because it is so unlike all that I perceive through my senses. It transcends the senses." - Mahatma Ghandi in his Spiritual Message to the World in 1931.

Doctor Kerr's staff at the hospice facility have witnessed many times the dying patient seeing visions. They will look up at the ceiling of their room, or straight ahead, often with arm outstretched. This activity is commonly followed by the patient talking to what it is seeing.

After this interaction, when the patient is asked who they were talking with or reaching for they will say that it was their dead spouse, or other relatives or close friends of theirs who are also deceased. Sometimes it may also be a dead pet of theirs. Whatever the case, it truly is a vision, and it can occur multiple times with the same patient.

Sam Kenison, comedienne, died due to complications of injuries received in an auto accident. His brother Bill was with Sam the night of the accident. Bill was driving a van with Sam's security team and Sam's opening act, while following Sam, who was driving his car, to a scheduled show in Vegas. Shortly after stopping for gas, Sam's car was involved in a head on accident.

His brother Bill immediately pulled the van alongside of Sam's wrecked car and jumped out of offer aid to Sam and his wife – who was the passenger in Sam's car. Bill proceeded to yank the car door open where he found Sam conscience and with a head injury due to his hitting the windshield. Shortly after, Sam was extricated from the car and was laid upon the side of the road.

Bill standing by Sam's side heard him say "I don't want to die. I don't want to die. And then a third time, I don't want to die". But then there was a pause as if Sam were listening to someone. Sam then stated "ok – ok – ok". Bill states that during this whole time, Sam was not talking to him, but talking to something else – something or someone that only Sam could see. Bill noted that after Sam uttered the three (3) oks', he took his last breath.

https://www.kinison.com/bill-kinison-sam-kinisons-last-words-the-truth-behind-his-final-moments/

Sam saw something that night, something that as his brother Bill stated, "he negotiated with" and accepted the final outcome – his own death, and as a result, Sam's vision directed and guided him on his final journey.

One has a choice here to decide if the vision was just a hallucination of Sam's brought about by the accident, or was it something more. In the final analysis you need to also consider the countless others who have had these types of visions and ask yourself – were all of these visions' mere hallucinations or something more – perhaps, as I believe, the Veil being thinner than we imagine.

2.2 VISITATION DREAMS, AND MY BROTHER'S DEATH

This book would not be complete without talking about having dreams with departed loved ones in them. Visitation Dreams as they are called, are a form of afterlife contact that our deceased loved ones may use to communicate with us from the other side. Many people, in many cultures from around the globe have reported having these experiences (see Appendix 3).

A visitation dream is described as a hyper-intensive dream where a deceased soul or loved one visits you. People who experience a visitation dream claim the dream's intensity feels real and they can remember very vivid details.

"Scientists cannot answer the question of whether these dreams are a way of communicating with the deceased or just an expression of our deepest desires," but at a conference of "The Compassionate Friends" that takes place every year, and is devoted to parents whose children have died, one of the main organizers and presenters, Charles Blow stated "**A dream of a deceased relative or friend is a gift. Do not delve into the analysis, just accept it with gratitude**." https://www.learning-

65

mind.com/why-do-our-deceased-loved-ones-come-in-our-
dreams/

Visitation dreams can occur for several reasons such as:

- A loved one has recently passed and they "show up" in the dream to notify the dreamer that his or her soul is okay.
- A soul needs closure and needs to communicate their feelings to answer or resolve something that happened during their physical life.
- A soul visits you to inform you of a problem or clue to living a better life. Often when we are lost in life the spirit world shows up to direct us to the "right" path.
- The soul is there to provide comfort and love during a rough time to assure you that everything will be okay. This also occurs for those who are grieving. The soul wants you to know that they are okay.
- A soul may visit just to visit. If they've been on your mind a soul may pop up to show their presence or strengthen your memories of them.

My wife and I have each had what are described as 'Visitation Dreams'. These dreams are usually vivid, and lifelike, and unlike regular dreams we feel comforted and/or somewhat directed. When we awake, we may totally understand the message given, or feel renewed in a way that can now lead us to find the answers we are seeking. For us, these were uncommon visits that had taken place, visits we were glad to have had.

We have had several members of our families pass away over the 40+ years that my wife and I have been married. While on our honeymoon my dad unexpectedly passed, two years later my wife's brother passed away as a result of a motorcycle accident. Many years later my brother also unexpectedly passed and the cause of death was determined to be a heart valve issue that is hereditary in nature. Then within a three-year period of time we lost my wife's parents and my mother, all as a result of complications from falls in their older age.

After their deaths we began to notice that our departed relatives were showing up in our dreams and not necessarily right away, but within weeks after their passing. And not only did they show up in our dreams, but our daughter also mentioned that she too was paid a visit in her dreams too.

We were not in distress during those dreams, but instead the dreams were calming and relaxing, and as it turned out provided messages that needed to be delivered to us. For example, I had a very recent one where my departed brother Art, we called him Butch, came to me.

I was dreaming about walking around in a mall, and all of a sudden, my brother showed up and walked with me for a bit. The dream was very vibrant and Butch was wearing a blue and white striped Oxford button down shirt. And as we walked, we exchanged pleasantries and I think it was a dream where Butch just popped in to say hello. He appeared very happy and the whole experience made me feel very content, almost uplifted.

Thinking about this later on, and still to this day, I was reminded of all the times he and I would walk the mall at Christmas time. Besides working full time in my career, I had started a janitorial-maintenance business that saw me working in several mall stores, along with my brother, after hours cleaning and readying the stores for their next day's activity.

Often, at Christmas time, after our maintenance job was completed, we would wander the mall looking at all of the decorations, especially those in the center concourse. This was a great time of the year, and we would have conversations about Christmas, work, and life in general. Though this kept me away from my own family for many Saturday evenings, in some ways I really missed those times with my brother.

This was not the first visitation I had from Butch, but it was definitely another enjoyable one. However, there was a visitation I had from my mom shortly after her passing that still has me contemplating the meaning to this day.

2.3   END OF LIFE DREAMS AND THE PASSING OF OUR MOM'S

Depending upon your personal viewpoint, fortunately or unfortunately, I was very much involved with the passing of both my mother and mother-in-law. Neither of these occurrences were welcomed, but both were part of the circle of life.

My mother-in-law passed prior to my mom as a result of complications due to a fall she had taken at a nursing facility. She was aging and had bouts of dementia and as a result was in a nursing home. One day she took a fall getting out of bed and because of the injuries received from the fall, this was for her, her beginning into the afterlife.

Prior to the fall she would relate stories to my wife, her daughter, of visitors she had in her dreams. Vivid dreams that involved her brother, parents, and other relatives. She described in detail not only the dream and the spoken words, but also the feelings she was having, those being calmness, relaxed, fearless, and the tenderness or love.

This vivid detail was a surprise to us because up to then she was experiencing more absentmindedness, repeating of questions and stories often common in older age people with occurrences of dementia. However, these stories of her dreams were more exacting, with more life in her voicing as she would recall them.

The sense of calmness she displayed, and her acceptance of these dreams as being a showing of tenderness and love, gave to us a sense of acceptance of the inevitable. Her circle of life now nearing the end, and the welcoming for the next stage of eternal life.

Within a matter of a few months my mother-in-law passed. Having been there to see and be witness to the passing was one of both rejoice and sadness. We were glad and comforted that

69

we were there with her as she passed, but also sad to have to say our last goodbyes. Looking back on this event, we have found that **it is important to understand that last breaths are just as important as first breaths.**

With the nurse announcing the official time of death, my wife and I with tear filled eyes, lifted our glasses (which I had filled with some wine), and cheered to her mom's life! A life that her mom had lived on her terms, though at times trying, but a life lived as best as her mom could envision.

My own mom's death was also the result of a fall. My mom had lived alone in her home, and one evening she decided she wanted to get a snack from the fridge. When at the fridge her legs gave out and she went down hard.

At that time my mom weighed in at about 110 pounds, almost 5' and very frail. According to the doctor, mom had severe osteoporosis, and if you looked at a cross section of her bones, as the doctor told me – '**it would look like very holey Swiss cheese"**. This was not good, and given my mom's blood thinner medication, prescribed due to a previous mild stroke, if she ever was injured due to a fall or whatever, she was at the risk of further severe bleeding.

The fall mom took caused her to fracture her pelvis, and a few other bones, and gave her slight bleeding on the brain. With the ambulance called for her, mom was whisked away to the hospital. Immediately, my wife and I went into action and drove to her house to get her clothing and other necessities she would need for her hospital stay.

Arriving at the hospital we found mom being wheeled to her room after having had a second cat scan. We stayed with mom for a while, and she was in pretty good spirits, accepting of her condition, but also a bit upset and concerned of what was to be the next step in her recovery.

Because of the bleeding on the brain, the doctors agreed to stop the blood thinner medication until such time as the bleeding subsided. This was another step in what would lead to her journey to the other side, the afterlife.

We lived almost three hours away from mom and though my current workload enabled me to stay with her for a while, my wife had to return home to provide caring for our grandkids. During my stay, mom related a few stories of how when her second husband Louie passed, that before he passed, he had dreams of past relatives – vivid dreams and would ask for the person when he became lucid. Mom stated that she too had seen past relatives in her dreams, though she did not state to me who they were. Mom did not talk much about her own family life, and if we were to ask about our heritage her response was – **"Why do you want to know about that – it's past history"**.

However, mom was a bit more talkative in her hospital bed and mentioned a few things that had happened to her in her childhood, mostly that their family was poor and mom had to work at an early age. She also mentioned things about her family that to date I had not known about, some good, some not. Mom also confessed that she had Louie come to her in a dream and state that it was time, and that it was going to be ok.

Mom's spirits were for the most part uplifted and she appeared comforted to some extent by these dreams. However, I could still sense that she was aware and perhaps thinking that the end maybe near in the same manner as it had happened with Louie.

Mom was progressing along, day by day, and by all signs appeared to be on the mend. It was going to be a fairly lengthy mending requiring maybe up to 6 months in rehab. Mom had gone through rehab once before for a fall she had taken years earlier so she had some idea of what it meant and although she was not looking forward to it, she was at least accepting of it.

The day came and mom was getting ready for release into rehab when the next major thing happened. Due in part to the order for her to stop taking the blood thinner medication, mom suffered another more massive stroke. Within seconds the hospital room filled with doctors, nurses, and anyone made necessary from a Code Blue Stat call to mom's hospital room.

There were a lot of people in this 10 x 10 hospital room, all moving about, talking in medical terms – almost like their own separate code words. I knew that this was not looking well for mom as the doctors worked feverishly to stem the stroke and its obvious impacts on her. And as soon as the many hospital personnel had first arrived into the room, almost all of them seemed to vanish, like roaches do when the lights are turned on. The remaining doctor advised that mom may not be able to recover from the stroke and all medical signs indicated that it was just a matter of time until she might leave this mortal soil. He also mentioned that mom's primary care doctor would be advised of this episodic event and he would be around to speak with me as soon as he could.

When mom's primary care doctor arrived at the hospital, I was further advised of mom's current condition and the various medical decisions I had available for her continued care. We discussed her frailness and I asked about her being fed intravenously, which the doctor did not advise. Instead, it was being made clear that I should accept her current state and try to make her as comfortable as possible in her remaining time with us. The primary care doctor and the doctors who were there when the stroke happened, were in agreement that I should begin to make end of life decisions for mom and that perhaps a morphine drip would be best at this time.

This is a most daunting decision as it truly is a decision that would make me the dreaded Reaper. With the morphine drip mom would be comfortable, well at least in no pain, but with no food or water it was just a matter of time until she would take her last breath, and I was the one having to make that decision.

Thoughts bouncing around within my head – was mom that close to dying, was she ready to go, could I actually make a life/death decision for her? Taking this decision to heart and weighing the doctor's observations and advice with what I thought was made necessary by mom's condition, reluctantly I chose to make her last moments as comfortable as I could. It was a choice I still think about and agonize over to this day. Mom took her last breath and passed on Valentine's Day.

Since mom's passing as I've mentioned, she has visited both my wife and I in our dreams. They were pleasant visits as my wife recalls. Visits that have often been about shared interest in hobbies and crafts, usually coming about when my wife had to make a decision about a direction to take with a quilt, crocheting, cooking or something else that they both had shared some passion for.

As was my mom, my wife is a crafter, having made many items such as quilts for the grandkids, crocheted items and ornaments for relatives. My wife is a pretty good cook as well, making many of my childhood favorites such as spaghetti and lasagna, fudge and fig cookies called Cuccidati, all of these favorite food items being made from recipe's handed down from my mom.

When my mom was alive and my wife ran into a problem while sewing, crocheting or cooking, she would call my mom for advice. When we would visit with mom, mom would show my wife what she was working on, or discuss a current recipe she had come upon, showing my wife one of the many cookbooks where she had found the various recipes. Whatever the item they discussed, both mom and my wife enjoyed their time together.

During these visitation dreams, as my wife recalls, mom would chat about the thing that my wife had been working on. When my wife would wake up, she would say that mom had come to her in her dream and told her how to fix something, how to proceed forward as next steps, and mention that it was a very nice visit.

Though scientists, and the medical professionals are still at odds as to what these dreams and visions are, for my wife and I we know that that having these dreams are Signs that indeed the Veil is thinner than we imagine.

"Every so often your loved ones will open the door from Heaven and visit you in a dream. Just to say Hello and to remind you they are still with you, just in a different way..."
– Matt Fraser (promotes himself as America's Top Physic Medium)

2.4   A Visitation Dream, and 'Not Enough'

Though my wife has had several good visitations from my departed mom, it has not been the same with me. Though I have had a few, there was this one that left me wondering aloud as to the meaning of it. The dream was calm and all, but mom spoke only a few words that I remembered when I awoke. Those words still consume some of my thinking capacity to this day.

During this dream mom was speaking to me and she said the words 'Not Enough'. That was what I remembered when I woke and wrote them down – just 'Not Enough'. Again, I wasn't troubled or had any kind of an eerie feeling from the dream, but I did not understand what she meant.

Perhaps maybe a little background might shed some light on my confusion. For the last maybe eight (8) or so years of mom's life she was living back in our hometown of Ilion NY. Mom was on a fixed income so I arranged to buy a house there and fix it up for her to live in. My brothers, Butch and Randy, helped in the remodeling efforts needed and when it was finished, we moved mom into the house.

Mom lived comfortably in that house and soon, with the help of her hair dresser, she found an organization that would have a care worker stop in a few times a week, check in on mom's health and do some light house work. Mom's needs were being met, and I handled all of her medical insurance needs, communicating with the various insurance agencies when needed. Mom had insurance coverage through Medicare, Humana and because of my father's military services, she also had benefits from the Veterans Administration, all of which I managed for her.

My hope was that mom would be comfortable in her golden years as she was by this time, in her mid-80's. Mom quickly settled into the house, having several friends stop by and see her during the week, and she continued with her weekly outings to the grocery store and to the beauty parlor. Most evenings you would find mom sitting in her favorite chair watching television, or sitting on the couch perhaps crocheting or knitting something.

Mom was careful walking as she had brittle bones. However, one day she fell at the house breaking her shoulder and wrist and knocking her leg bone out of its socket. After several hours of operation and several transfusions, mom would spend a few months in rehab before she was able to return to her home. During rehab my family and I visited mom, grandkids in tow, and this definitely made mom smile.

Soon mom was back in her house and once again tending to her daily needs, only now she struggled with her arm as it did not have the movement as it did before the accident. Over time that house proved to be too much for mom to live in safely, as it was a two-story house and mom was beginning to have trouble managing with the stairs.

Searching the 'for sales' in Ilion, I soon found another house for mom, where she could live on one floor. I bought that one, remodeling it as I had the first one, and moved mom into it.

Mom lived in that house for a few years and then late one evening I received a call from mom's hair dresser informing me that mom had taken another fall but that she did not want to go to the hospital. After some discussion we all convinced mom to go to the hospital, where they found she had once again broken some bones, which was going to require a hospital stay and again some rehab before she could return home. And as I mentioned earlier, this time mom would not make it back home as this was the beginning of the end. The complications from the injuries of the fall led to mom's passing.

While mom was in the hospital my wife and I visited and stayed with her, right up until the last breath she took. Family was with us during that time, my aunt, my sister Diane and her husband Mike, and my children. Others also came to visit her while she was in the hospital and mom would respond to their visiting as best she could.

The closer it was to mom's last breath, you would find her with her mouth open as she lay in bed, mostly sleeping as death came ever closer. Then there was another visitor, the hospital chaplain that stopped by and asked if there was anything she could do. We asked for a bedside prayer to be said, which she gladly obliged. During the prayer we all noticed that mom's mouth which had been open for hours, was then closed by her.

The prayer was said as we all stood with bowed heads, and within a half hour of the prayer, mom passed into the next realm. Comforted that mom was now out of pain, but saddened she was gone, we began to let family and friends know of her passing.

The following days found us making calls to various places that needed to know of mom's passing such as the insurance companies, Medicare, social security and veterans' administrations. Then we called the various cable and utility companies to cancel service at her house. Being that this was a small town, we also called the police department alerting them as to what had happened and how mom's house would remain empty until weekends, when my wife and I could travel back there and begin to clean, paint and ready the house for sale.

Thinking back on my visitation dream with mom, the words 'Not Enough' are now as it was then – confusing. Did I not do enough for her, did I not try hard enough to keep her alive in her last days? Was I not there enough, or did I not say I love you enough, or was mom saying that she did not say thanks enough, or is it still something more?

There is that part of me that second guesses the life and death decisions I had to make for mom. Trust me, seeing a loved one lying there in bed and knowing that there is nothing you can do to change the situation except to pray and make her ending as peaceful as possible – you then make the agonizing decision, as guided by the doctors, to agree to the morphine drip, that magical elixir necessary to ease any pain in their remaining life.

Agonizing and heart breaking as it was to see your mother lying there in pain, it was also unsettling to know that the order for the elixir that you just authorized was also an order given to end your own mom's life - not a situation I wish upon anyone.

Perhaps mom will pay another visit if she can, and perhaps too maybe she can tell me more information as to what she meant by – 'Not Enough'.   I still ponder today as to the meaning of those couple words. I'm not sure if I will ever be able to come to a conclusion that makes sense to me, that makes me comfortable, that is until the time we meet each other again – on the other side of the Veil.

"For there is no death, only transition from the physical to the spiritual plane." Edgar Cayce reading 136 - 33

3 GROUPING THREE: OBJECTS AND SMELLS

Have you had an inanimate object suddenly turn on, or move on its own? Have you had a sudden smell come about you and there was no logical explanation as to why it occurred? What about having a lost object just show up after extensive searching proved fruitless?

Within this section will be stories that specifically deal with Signs as delivered through objects and via smells. And not all of these signs are necessarily understood upon receipt and sometimes the sign may be very personal and only understood by the recipient.

3.1 A MISSING EARRING, AND A SPECIAL VISIT?

Over the summer of 2020, our very best friends Brad and Louise Bixby came for a visit and stayed with us for a few days. During this time, we experienced a Sign that involved an inanimate object, and it was witnessed by the four of us. We believe this Sign had come from a departed loved one who we believe was my mom. I'd like to set the stage a bit here and present what is called the backstory.

Early in 2019, on Valentine's Day, my mom who was 91, had passed away as the result of complications from a fall she had two weeks prior. She had fallen at home, and broke some bones and it was also discovered that she had bleeding on the brain, and the medical precautions to stop this bleeding may have led to the stroke that eventually ended her life.

This was a sad time for us as we saw the last of our maternal parents passing. My wife had lost her dad two years prior and her mom one year prior. My dad had passed away suddenly at the age of 52, some four decades earlier. Now that my mom was gone, we were now officially the 'Old People' as my wife and I would tell each other.

I previously mentioned that over the many years of our marriage, my wife and my mom were able to bond over recipes for cooking and baking, and especially their love for things that are crafty.

My mom had a ton of fabric, yarn and other craft items in her house and whenever we would visit with her, my wife and mom would spend time discussing their latest craft. I was most likely fixing things, changing the smoke detector batteries, or running to the store for some part for something else needing to be fixed. Overall, my job during these visits was making sure the house was in good repair, and going to the store for whatever supply or grocery item that was needed.

Now back to the story. While the Bixbys were visiting with us, we had some planned events including going to some of the many local museums, going out to eat, or simply having game night at the house, where we would relax and share a drink or two.

One of the events we had planned was a visit to **The Genesee Country Museum** in Mumford NY – a museum that has full scale villages laid out in three (3) different time periods representing structures as they would have been found during the 1700's, 1800's, and 1900's. This is a fun place to walk through the many homes and businesses of the time periods while reminiscing of by-gone eras.

The night before the visit to the museum, we had a casual dinner, followed by desert and drinks, and then a game of Dominoes. This is where the stage was set for the next Sign that would be presented to us.

After dinner, and the clearing of the kitchen table, I proceeded to get the Dominoes game from the closet. With the drinks refreshed we all sat down to the kitchen table, ready for a friendly, but somewhat competitive game night.

During the game, my wife and I sat on one side of the table and the Bixby's sat across from us on the other side. This enabled all of us to see the game board and gave us plenty of room to lay out our dominoes. We played several rounds and really enjoyed the evening festivities – good food, good drink and good friends! What's not to like?

We had played a few rounds of the game and were now into the next. All the while my wife was fiddling a bit with one of her earrings. This was a habit she had whenever she was in deep thought about things – in this case her next move(s). However, while fiddling around with the earring it came off from its backing and landed on what we thought was the floor. We temporarily halted the game while my wife looked for her earring. Only this is where things were about to get very interesting.

My wife looked and looked and could not find the earring, and soon we all found ourselves joining in the hunt for this run away earring. We searched the floor, and the seating around the table – no luck. We searched the floor beneath the kitchen island, which is about five (5) feet away from the kitchen table, again no luck. By the way this earing was about one and half inches long so not something that was easily missed. After we had searched everywhere we could think to, we agreed to stop searching and resume the game.

That evening upon retiring for the night, my wife shook out the clothes she had been wearing, and no earring. She even brushed her hair vigorously – again no earring. My wife was feeling bad that she could not find the earring as it had been a gift to her and she did not want to lose it. I consoled her not to worry, that it would show up, and with the evening ending we shut off the lights and headed off to sleep.

The next morning, bright and early, we all sat down to breakfast at the kitchen island with coffee, toast, eggs, bacon and the like – loading up for our day of walking around the museum. When the breakfast was finished and before leaving the house, we all cleaned up the kitchen, taking care of the dishes and wiping down the island counter. And with the breakfast chores all complete we headed out for a fun-filled day.

The Museum was great to visit and we enjoyed the walk down memory lane. The blacksmith told of how iron shoes were made and demonstrated the same. The tin smith talked about his profession, and the ladies of one of the early homes talked about cheese making, and food preservation. After a bit of lunch, and further village house viewing we were ready for a nice dinner and relaxing back at our house.

It was now 5pm when we arrived back home, pulling the car into the garage and gathering our belongings of the day. I was the first to the back door, unlocking it and entering the back hallway with the others right behind.   Upon entering the kitchen my wife remarked – "hey hon, thanks so much for finding my earring". This statement caught me a bit off guard as I had not found anything as I just walked into the kitchen mere seconds before her.

I turned to her and asked what she meant as I had not found anything yet. She said, what do you mean – immediately pointing to the kitchen island, and all eyes went there and saw – that there sitting upon the island in plain sight, the same island we had just sat at for our breakfast, was in fact her lost earring.

All of a sudden, our heads turned towards one another with puzzled looks upon our faces, and remarks of 'how could that be'? The earring was not there at breakfast, we had cleared and wiped down the island before we left for the day, and no one else had been in the house while we were gone.

This earring had us wondering aloud how it could have been placed on the counter. Had the four of us been blind to it last night and at breakfast? How could we not have seen it when we cleaned up after breakfast and more importantly who could have placed it there. After all, how could my wife have flicked it there from her ear (quite some distance from where we were sitting), and it having landed on the island without making a sound. So, what were we now seeing and experiencing.

We began to think out loud and of course either my wife or I mentioned that we have had other occurrences like this in our life. Things that we just could not explain, things that have often left us wondering.

Louise commented that she too has had these types of events, and with that she grabbed her purse and took from it a small Red Cardinal charm, accompanied with a piece of paper with writing on it. She then took the charm and placed it on the island where the earring was found.

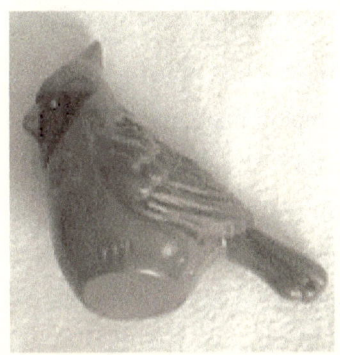

Here is a picture of the cardinal that Louise took from her purse and placed in the area of where the earring was found. The writing upon the paper read, *"This little cardinal will bring good luck to you, with renewal and faith in all that you do. Find your life song, show gratitude each day; believe and have hope, the cardinal will lead the way."* A. S. Waldrop

I had mentioned my mom earlier and the relationship she had with my wife, but what I had not told you yet, and as I too was about to find out, was that the earrings that my wife was wearing, the one that was then lost but then found sitting on the island counter the next day, the one that I mentioned had been a gift to my wife, was in fact a gift from my mom.

Had this been a Sign that we had been paid a visit by my departed mom? Well maybe. To this day we have found no other logical explanation as to what had transpired to enable the lost earring to show up on the kitchen island, the same place we had breakfast, and same island counter we had cleared and wiped down afterwards.

That morning of eating at the island counter and not seeing the earring, then coming back home and finding the earring sitting upon the island counter, was indeed one of the more interesting occurrences of this type that my wife and I have experienced. And to have witnesses, the Bixby's present to both see and collaborate our story, well that made this Sign that much more remarkable and significant.

You might ask why, after finding the earring, Louise then placed a cardinal charm onto the island in the very area where the earring was found. Well, it is often said that when a cardinal appears a lost loved one is near. And another more religious saying is that "when cardinals appear, an angel is near". I cannot argue the merits of this with what we had all experienced. I will be speaking more about the meaning of Red Cardinals later in the book. For now, I have no other explanation for the erring to be found on the island. I am content in thinking that indeed mom had paid us a visit, a Sign that she is always nearby, and a sign that indeed the Veil is thinner than we imagine!

3.2 A DEATH, A FUNERAL, AND CIGARETTE SMOKE

The year was 2010 and I was on a business trip, a sales conference in Florida. My colleagues and I were in a car heading out for dinner and to discuss what tasks we were all going to be doing at the event the next day. We had no sooner left the hotel parking lot when I received a devastating phone call from my wife informing me that my brother Butch – had passed away.

My brother was within days of turning 59 and his passing was a shock to our family. Needless to say, I arranged for the first flight home, arriving home early the next day, where my wife picked me up from the airport. While on the drive home she began telling me of the consequences leading up to my brother's death.

My brother was found face down in his backyard, by a neighbor who then notified the police. The police found my brother near his lawn mower with the lawn partially mowed. Their assumption was that he died while mowing the lawn, but because this was what they called an unattended death – an autopsy would need to be performed to validate the cause of death; and of course, based on the cause – what if any additional police action might be necessary.

The autopsy results showed that my brother died from natural causes, a faulty heart valve that we would come to realize was hereditary. My dad had suffered what was called a massive heart attack and passed away in 1976, three (3) months shy of 52 years of age. And my next older brother Lon had his heart valve replaced years prior to my brother Butch's death. At the time we were advised that there was not enough evidence to link my brother Lon's heart valve issue with my dad's heart attack. In fact, we were explicitly told that the heart valve issue was not hereditary.

Once Butch's autopsy was performed and the results known, as soon as I could I made arrangements to see a cardiologist. Needless to say, after reviewing all of the family's heart events and my current concerns with the cardiologist, he then told me the following: first thing he stated is that heart valve issues can indeed be hereditary in nature, and second that he wanted me to have a stress test and echocardiogram to see if I might have the same issue. Long story short – I do, and since that time I have been under cardiologist care with yearly exams.

Butch's funeral and services were held in our hometown of Ilion NY and a reception gathering was held at my mom's home following his funeral services. After the services I drove my wife and mom, back to mom's house. During the lull before the reception began, we sat in mom's living room making small talk about Butch and the services. All of a sudden, one by one, we began to smell cigarette smoke. This was very odd, as none of us smoked and no one had been in my mom's house who did smoke.

Looking at each other, we began commenting on the cigarette smell. I got up to check around the house to see where this cigarette smoke smell might be coming from, no one was outside, and no one else was in the house – so where was this cigarette smoke smell coming from?

It dawned on all of us almost at the same time, that this had to be a Sign from Butch. Butch smoked, and not only that – so had my dad. Was this Butch visiting us? Was this perhaps both

Butch and Dad visiting us? Was this their way of giving us comfort that they were together in the afterlife? Although we were all still very sad of my brother's passing, we did take comfort in the belief that he was still there with us, communicating to us in the only way he could.

During a more recent get-together with my younger sister Diane and her husband Mike, we were discussing my writing of this book and what some of the chapter details were going to be. During the discussion about this particular event, my sister began to tell us of what she believed was an encounter she had with Butch after his death.

Mom did not take the untimely passing of Butch very well. This was her son, her child, and as they say the worst kind of death is when a parent loses a child. To aid in her comfort, my sister would visit with mom and help her however she could.

During one of those visits, mom had asked Diane to go upstairs and retrieve an item from her craft room. Mom being big into crafts, sewing, knitting, crocheting, etc., was currently working on a project and needed the item that she had asked Diane to get for her.

The stairs to the second floor had a landing midway up where you would then make a ninety (90) degree turn to continue up to the second floor. When Diane was walking up the stairs and reached the landing, just as she was about to make the turn, she began to smell cigarette smoke. She immediately looked around and nobody else was there. However, as she told us the story, she said that at that moment of smelling smoke she had a great sense of calm come over her, and she said 'Butch is that you'?

Once again for some unexplained reason there was that smell of cigarette smoke in moms house with no one around. Over the several years that mom lived in that house, my wife and I visited regularly, and before mom moved into that house, my brother' Butch and Randy, along with my wife and I, spent several weekends remodeling it. Never once had any of us encountered the smell of cigarette smoke.

Finding no other logical reason for the smelling of cigarette smoke, especially when no one was smoking, we were left with the question of what was causing it to occur. Our conclusion – we truly believed this was indeed a Sign that Butch was with us and communicating in a manner that he knew we would understand.

For me, my wife and my sister these occurrences where truly Signs that brought us great calmness. Demonstrating once again that the Veil is thinner than we imagine!

"Death is not an ending, but a symbol of movement along the path upon which we are all traveling. As it may be painful to lose contact with the physical aspect of the one we love, the Spirit can never be lost. We have been and always will be a part of each other." – John Denver

3.3 Did You Just Say 'Stupid Jerk'?

My wife and I live in Rush NY, a suburb south of Rochester, and Butch lived about 15 miles north of us. We would have get-togethers for cook-outs, birthdays, holidays and the like, and Butch was always a welcomed part of those gatherings.

Butch never married, and he had always worked. He did find time for his hobbies of photography and remodeling his home (which he was very proud of). I would sometimes help him with his remodeling tasks, while sharing a beer or two, and having good conversations. And it's these hobbies that would tie into other Signs that I and others have personally experienced.

It was hard for me to accept my brother's untimely passing, and I still find myself in disbelief today. Butch was only 6 years older than me, and it seemed he could never really catch a break in life. He worked really hard, but did not make a lot of money for his efforts. Though he did not lack for the basics of life, it always seemed that just as he had some finances ahead, or was about to receive a large overtime check or other such remuneration from work, his car would break down, or his house needed a major repair – such as the furnace breaking, or something else out of the ordinary; a not planned for type expense would swoop in and snatch his nest egg – putting him further behind in his financial goals.

When Butch first moved to Rochester he stayed with my family. Until he had a full time job, he assisting me in a side-line business I had started. He would also help around the house by assisting me with some of my own house remodeling tasks, and would on occasion mow the yard. He would do this not because we asked, but because it was his way to pay back our hospitality.

After Butch moved out, he continued to save until he had enough to buy his house. Butch was very excited about his house, and though it was not yet his castle, he had plans for the remodeling, and he would continue those remodeling tasks even up to the time of his death, never having seen the finished home he had worked so hard to achieve.

Upon Butch's passing, one of the items I inherited from him was a plastic novelty device, called '**The Final Word**' that he had purchased in a store called Spencer's Gifts, located in our local mall. This item fit in your hand and was battery operated.

Upon pushing in the button on the side of the device, it would utter one of 4 different insensitive remarks to the operator. The remarks that came from this device were sayings of 'Stupid Jerk', 'You're a Dope', 'You're an Idiot' and 'Drop Dead'. It is this device that is at the center of the Sign I was to receive.

On occasion when I would go to Butch's house he would have that device near at hand, and at the opportune moment he would press the button and I would hear...**'Stupid Jerk'**. Of course, we'd get a chuckle out of it and soon we would be on our way to the next remodeling task, or off to work on my sideline business.

Then there were those times that I just went there for a visit. We'd grab a beer, or a coffee, and just sit and chat about life in general, or a work event, or whatever 'crap' (as we would call it) was on the news. Butch and I were pretty close and his death came as a big shock for me and one I did not easily accept.

At the time of his passing, I was working for the Xerox corporation and I had a home office that I worked out of. I was a technical project manager and would often travel for business. When I was not traveling for business, I could then be found conducting my project work from my home office.

Business travel and working from a home office is not as glamorous as it may sound. Though I must admit that the winter commutes that I no longer had to endure on New York state roads did offer some reward for the many long hours of work that I would experience on an almost daily basis.

It was now the late fall season and I was working in my home office, tiring away on what I am sure were a few projects needing to be wrapped up before year's end. With Xerox, as most private corporations I would imagine, the end of the year events were a time of hustle and bustle especially given the shortened timeframe due to the many holidays over the last three months of the year. Stress levels amongst the sales people to close their sales cycles and management's constant hovering over them to understand what they may need to do so, often led to some very tight deadlines, and short tempers.

My job as a technical project manager was to assist the sales teams with their presales and ongoing sales cycle activities in developing the outsourcing solutions that met the customer's need. Then once the account was sold, I would then project manage the installation of the outsourcing solution we had sold to the client. Therefore, end of year activity for me was often one of long hours necessitated by tight timelines brought on by multiple project deadlines. And of course, with that came the accompanied stress of it all.

One day, about midmorning while I was working away, then out of the blue I heard that plastic novelty item sound off with **'Stupid Jerk'**, that very same familiar sound I had heard on so many of my visits to see Butch at his house! '**What the heck was that**', I wondered to myself, and getting up from my chair I crossed the room to the bookcase where the device was resting.

96

I picked up the device and I just looked at it, examining it in a way that maybe I was anticipating it sounding off again.

How could that have sounded off as it required the pressing of the button to get the device to play. I tried to make the device sound off without pushing in the button on the side, but it would not play. Shaking the device had no effect on making it play. I placed it back on the bookcase and then I bumped the bookcase in an effort to make it play – nothing. Jumping up and down near the bookcase also had no effect on the device to play. OK, so what then had caused the device to play and sound off with **'Stupid Jerk'**? And with four (4) different saying on the device, why did it say 'Stupid Jerk'?

I was thinking about it for a moment, and I said out loud – **"Butch, was that you"– are you playing around with me today"?** I do remember feeling a sense of calm, and almost a relaxed feeling like that of having had a good belly laugh. While thinking about what just occurred, I placed the device back on the bookcase and went back and resumed my work.

That night over dinner I recounted the happenings of earlier that day. My wife listened with both amazement and a somewhat **'yeah so what's so unusual about that'** attitude. And as she stated "after all you know our past loved ones have visited before" and with that she recounted some stories of the many times we have thought that we were visited by one of our departed loved ones.

To this day I cannot explain a logical reason as to why that device played that day, sounding off without human intervention, and saying '**Stupid Jerk**'. That device has been in my office since I had received it and other than that day, I can tell you I have not heard another sound from it since.

For me this was a Sign, for why else would it have played? What other force would have caused this to play when no one pressed the play button? I am left with no other logical reasoning that makes any sense, let alone is repeatable.

Once again, I truly believe that the Veil is indeed thinner than we imagine.

3.4 GRANDMOTHER, GRANDCHILDREN AND CANDY

We have shared some of these stories with our family and close friends. I will admit that we are cautious as to who we share them with as we do not want everyone to think we might be a little off our rocker! However, I am happy to say that once we do, it is almost like a flood gate opens up and our family and friends begin to share their stories with us. They are thankful to share their stories and not think that they were perhaps delusional, crazy or otherwise ready to be committed.

When we shared these stories with our daughter, though she was a bit skeptical at first, she told us of the experiences she recently had that make her no longer even question our Sign stories. Our daughter's own Sign story was something that involved her very recently departed mother-in-law.

When our daughter's children (our grandkids) would visit with their other grandparents, the grandmother would give the grandkids a small wrapped piece of candy, which the grandkids loved to receive. The wrapper of the candy was unique in that it had a picture of a cardinal and the words 'Red Bird' written on it.

My daughter's mother-in-law passed in October of 2022, and this was a bit of a shock as she had been battling breast cancer, and after treatment for that she was told that the breast cancer was gone. However, a couple weeks after receiving news of her end of breast cancer, she noticed that she was having trouble breathing and with that she went back into the hospital for tests. These new tests revealed that she had cancer in her lungs and that the prognosis was a relatively few weeks of life remaining.

The last days of her life were spent at her house, comforted by her family, friends and pets. She lived for a couple more weeks and passed in the presence of her family. Though it was comforting for them to be present during this time, her passing was deeply and emotionally felt by them.

Not long after her passing our daughter and grandkids were finding candy wrappers, from the candy that the grandmother would give to the grandkids, showing up in their house and their car. For example, one morning as my daughter was heading to her children's bedroom to wake them, there on the floor near one of the bedroom doors was a candy wrapper. Then on another day she found a wrapper in one of her daughter's bedrooms, and recently she found a wrapper in their car. And the latest sighting was that our daughter and grandkids were visiting with us and our daughter went to grab a Kleenex from her coat and when she did one of the candy wrappers fell out.

Coincidence – perhaps, but her mother-in-law passed away three (3) months prior and there has not been any more of the candy purchased in that time, and especially no one to give out that candy. And of course, my daughter has cleaned her house and would have seen the wrapper lying on the floor before now. So where did the wrappers come from?

Just in case you are thinking the children had hidden the candy and are just now eating it, well they were 4 and 6 years old at this time, and as our daughter has told us – they would eat the candy as soon as they got it. Again, we have to ponder the question of where did those wrappers come from, and how did they get into the places where they were found?

By the way, our grandkids have horses and their dad and his mom have had horses all their lives. The grandkids loved spending time around with their grandma as she tended the horses, and had a very good relationship with her as a result. And it is my opinion that these wrappers were their deceased grandma's way of communicating with her son's family in the only way she knows how.

And another thing to consider is the picture on the wrapper of the red bird candy – a Cardinal. There's a belief that seeing a cardinal after the loss of a beloved person symbolizes a visit from the other side, that you're receiving a message that the soul of the deceased person is still with you and you're not alone in this world. Further it is said that a red cardinal appears in your enclosure after the death of a beloved person, it's not a coincidence and you need to take these messages seriously.

The red cardinal has come to symbolize eternal flame and immortality, a visit from heaven of a passed loved one, an angel. And the red color of the cardinal's feathers is the ultimate symbol of love. Think about Valentine's Day and how the color red is ubiquitous at that time as the symbol of love.

A simple candy wrapper, but perhaps a profound statement of love. A message, perhaps, that we do not perish into nothingness, that our souls are endless and we can still be around to help with a gentle nudge or a message delivered in a candy wrapper. Coincidence maybe, but in my view, these wrappers are indeed Signs, Signs that the Veil is thinner than we imagine.

3.5 A FRAMED PICTURE, A PLACARD AND A HOSPITAL ER

Marjorie Longley Graham, Boofie as we all called her, was a high school classmate of mine and has been a great friend over the years. Boofie agreed to share a few stories of her own personal experiences with – as she describes them, visits from the beyond. She further states that these stories are so easy to recall, as these encounters occurred with witnesses' present!

Thank you very much Boofie for being willing to share your personal stories.

Boofie's stories in her words:

> The **first, most vivid and profound physical Sign** was provided by my recently deceased father. My husband and I traveled to Minnesota, from our home in California, to participate in my dad's memorial service. When all of the other guests left the repast, we stayed in the living room of my father's home talking quite seriously about some details we did not agree upon. Ok, yes, my husband and I we were in a debate, hmm, an argument actually, over the disappearance of dad's will – an incredibly convenient affair for my step mother!

The living room contained two (2) sofas and an antique "queen's" chair richly upholstered in mohair. A large credenza stood in front of a series of 3 windows, all closed for the air conditioner to be efficient as the weather was steamy hot. On the credenza were 8 to 10 framed photos that were important to my father.

While in the middle of our heated discussion something amazing happened. A single framed photo flew up off the credenza and out into the middle of the living room!!! Only that single photo, all others remained immobile and unmoved, it was as if only this single photo wanted our attention. It was late and no one else was awake in the house. I immediately got up to retrieve and replace the photo onto the credenza, and to take a closer look, trying to decipher how it flew up and over on its own!!

Upon examining the photo, I discovered that it was the one with my father, myself, and my husband Ron at Ron's Executive Master of Business Administration (EMBA) graduation ceremony at Pepperdine's Graziadio school of Business. Dad had been so excited and proud that day to join us in celebration.

Still wondering how this framed picture flew off the credenza had me thinking that perhaps this was Dad's way of sending us a message, one of "stop arguing, the 'will' really does not matter", or "look, this is a bigger deal – there is life after death, here is a Sign of proof

Boof!" Whatever its message I knew one thing for sure
– I felt that at that time dad was there and watching over
us.

The **second incredible Sign** involved my genealogical
research for our American Revolutionary Patriots. For
nearly 2 years my final search was for a specific church
in PA that held the last amount of proof required to link
family generations 8, 7, & 6. My mission had become
intensely personal and though I knew the church name,
and that the baptisms I searched for were all listed in
this one book, that book was nowhere to be found!

I was spending every Wednesday at the Mormon Library
in Santa Monica, in the Pennsylvania section scouring
all available records, only to find myself coming up
empty-handed. I was so determined to find this
information that I had even taken a trip to the area in
Pennsylvania where this church had once existed, and I
still did not find the baptismal records for the period in
our history that I had so required.

One final day of searching the Mormon Library, I
grabbed a book from the library shelf, and placed the
brightly colored placard, as I had been so often
instructed to do, as a place holder for the removed book.
These are long placards, and after a couple of years
were easily used, with so much practice. As I began
walking away, I and several others who were close by,

heard a "thunk". Turning around to see what made that noise, I noticed the placard that I had just placed on the shelf was now laying upon the floor!

Bending over to pick up the placard, and to replace it properly back on to the shelf above, I was dumbfounded as to what the placard had landed in front of! YEP, there on the shelf in front of the placard was the elusive publication that contained the specific church records I had been searching for nearly two (2) years to find!!!

Not certain as to which one of my departed family members had made this clear and present action which solved our family lineage, but you can imagine the elated feeling, and my belief that there was divine intervention in this discovery! I firmly believe if one is open to receive, there are many visits to each of us, especially when in need. Long ago these visits were explained by having "guardian angels", who are we to doubt?

That reminds me of another time *- a very intense – experience I had with many eye witnesses!!*

I volunteered in the emergency room (ER) at Saint John's Hospital in Santa Monica California. I was working the afternoon shift and it was a typical busy time. A man was brought in by ambulance, rushed into a room where monitors were immediately attached to him. Apparently, he was suffering a massive heart attack.

Within the hour of his arrival a very strange and bewildering phenomena had taken place. A very strong rush of ice cold air flew out of the room he was occupying, proceeded to go through the security door into the waiting area and then all of a sudden, the electronic double entrance doors opened and the cold air proceeded to leave the building through the open doors!!!!!

The several people around who had witnessed this all looked at each other in amazement. What was that cold air all about, and how did those doors open as those particular doors do not open without activation by a "body" or a wheelchair!

While reviewing the circumstances that had just happened, we discovered that at the very moment the frozen air traveled through our waiting room and out of the building, the man who had been brought into the ER and occupied the room that the cold air emanated from had just died!

What can one make of these experiences? You have to ask the questions and seek the answers. Why did the picture fly off the credenza and out into the center of the room? Why did the placard fall to the floor in front of the very book Boofie had been tirelessly searching for? And what was causing that cold air to flow out of the room of a deceased person and to make the doors open up when it takes something physical to do so?

My response throughout the stories presented thus far, has been that these are all Signs. Signs that we are not alone, that there is more here that we need to be open to receiving. Could it be our departed loved ones, maybe something Angelic or Devine in nature? Perhaps it is nothing more than our imagination – but then again there are many witnesses to these 'imaginations', so then what explains that?

I do not pretend to have all the answers, however the more people I have spoken with doing my research for this book, I am more and more convinced that indeed the Veil is thinner than we can imagine.

The only way of finding the limits of the possible is by going beyond them into the impossible. – Arthur C. Clarke

3.6   A STEP-FATHER, A VISIT, AND A PICTURE

My wife Sharon had a Signs encountered very recent that involved the passing of her step-father Jim (yes, stepfather had same name as her biological dad). Jim passed away December 9, 2022, after a long life as he was then 92.

For the last 17 years of his life, Jim lived in Washington state with Sharon's sister's family. Jim was a nice person, easy to talk to, loved the outdoors and was an avid sports watcher. When Jim was younger, he worked for United Airlines as an airline mechanic, and had worked out of a few locations around the country. Jim married Sharon's mom in 1972 when Sharon was only 13, and they built a home in Rosemount, Minnesota.

Jim would take the family on many outings, and Sharon has fond memories of them, including him taking her and her sister on fishing trips. Jim was also known for his many fun stories that he would tell of his adventures, and some of the famous people he met while working at the airport – especially the sports players. Though as I was told, Jim also had a very pleasant encounter with Jacklyn Kennedy Onassis over a cup of coffee.

After Jim retired from Unites Airlines, he spent the summers working in Yosemite National Park, at a camping resort there, as an all-around handy man, tour guide, friend and helper to the campers. Jim loved this job and enjoyed his encounters with nature and the campers. Then as the fall season and the snows came to the park, Jim would prep and close down the campsites, and afterwards return to Sharon's sister's residence in Washington state.

Over the years Sharon and I have visited all of them in Washington, and we would always enjoy the time we spent there. A year ago, right after covid, Sharon took a solo trip to see her sister's family and Jim. They had a great time, relaxing, telling stories and going out to eat, and taking many pictures with the family. Upon her return, Sharon told me she could see that

Jim was not as active as he used to be and that he was slowing down. During that solo visit Jim had turned 91 years of age.

Over the last couple years Jim's health had faltered, gradually deteriorating until late in 2022 where he took a turn for the worst, not wanting much to eat, and spending more time sleeping than was ever typical. Then on December 9, 2022 Jim passed of natural causes. Sharon's family, though expecting this was coming sooner than later, were certainly grief stricken by this.

Though understanding that Jim was now out of any pain, and that he was probably telling stories of his many adventures to fellow angels, Sharon deeply felt the news of his passing and was definitely grieving. And though as of this writing, it's only been a short time since his passing, I can see that with a Sign Sharon recently received, she has begun her transition into the acceptance stage of grieving. That unexpected Sign she received had been delivered via her iPhone.

Typical for most iPhones there are several apps that come standard with the phone setup and others you can purchase. Sharon's iPhone has many apps with some that alert her with information as example, she receives her Bible Quote of the Day, and she has an app to help her track and report on her Fitbit steps. And there is one other feature that this phone has, and that is that it shows random past memories as the 'picture of the day'. This is a feature that Sharon likes a lot as it gives her great joy seeing the pictures and reliving the memories.

The day after Jim's passing the 'picture of the day' displayed on the iPhone was a photograph showing Sharon, her sister, and Jim; a photo that was taken at Sharon's mom's memorial that had been held two years earlier in Michigan. Coincidence, well maybe, or perhaps a Sign from Jim. A Sign indicating that he was OK, that he was still around watching over them, and they should remember the love he had for them.

Jim was now at peace and with that photo showing up on Sharon's iPhone, the day after his passing, was just the Sign she needed to begin her journey into the process of acceptance. A Sign, perhaps, that shows that indeed the Veil is thinner than we imagine.

"To live in the hearts we leave behind is not to die." Thomas Campbell

4 GROUPING FOUR: ASKING FOR HELP

Have you ever wondered aloud, or prayed aloud, about not finding something, only to then have the object found? How about wondering if you did a good job for someone, even asking aloud if you did. What if that someone you were wondering about doing a good job for was deceased, and you never found out how they thought about the job you did.

Within this section will be stories that highlight how we can ask for help, or for an answer to a question, and in doing so – receive the Sign. Again, some of these signs may not be understood upon receipt, and sometimes the sign may be very personal and only understood by the recipient.

4.1 A MISSING CHUCK KEY, AND MY PATIENCE

During the first decade of our marriage, we managed through having two children, buying a house, finishing my college degree while my wife was working on finishing hers. On the not so good side we had also managed through two sudden and unexpected deaths in our families that caused us to lose both my father and my wife's brother.

These deaths were shocks to our family, and definitely tested our faith. But with time we accepted what had occurred, and it

helped us to see life in different ways. It was also during this
time that one of our earliest Signs that my wife and I remember
having were of these departed loved ones.

When you lose a loved one, sometimes you may find yourself
just talking to them as if they were still there. You may be asking
them questions, wondering out loud, and just chatting with them
as you would to a friend. You might ask out loud – what would
you do if...or how would you fix this dad...etc... If you were to
ask me if they listen, well my response would be – oh heck yeah
they do!

Being a bit of a handy-man type person, I often take care of the
maintenance chores about the house. Fixing broken items,
repairing leaking faucets, building a deck, finishing a room in the
basement, and other such household 'fix up' tasks and remodels.
To accomplish all of this it was necessary to have the proper
tools such as screwdrivers, saws, drills, wrenches, hammers,
and the assorted electric, battery, gas and air powered tools too.

The drill is an essential component and has a wide range of uses
around the house. From drilling a hole, to screwing/unscrewing
a screw, to sanding or grinding – there are a host of attachments
for the common drill. With most all electric drills of that time, you
needed a chuck key. The chuck key was necessary in order to
loosen and tighten the chuck, which is the part of the drill that
holds tight to the drill bit or other attachment.

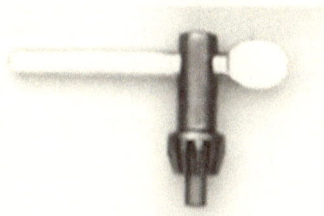

This is a picture of a chuck key.

With some drills there is a leather or rubber strap that would attach to the electrical cord of the drill, that you would then attach the chuck key to so as not to lose it. For most battery-operated drills of the time, the chuck key was often found in a molded slot in the handle of the drill where you would store the chuck key and thereby having it at the ready and making sure not to lose it.

Today's more modern and powerful drills, especially the newer battery-operated ones, have a hand loosening and tightening chuck, thereby eliminating the need for a chuck key altogether.

One day I found myself in need of a drill to accomplish a specific household task. I had the drill and the drill bit at hand, but for the life of me I could not find the chuck key. I began searching the work bench, the parts drawer, my tool box, even our miscellaneous drawer where we would put odds and ends aka our junk drawer, containing things of need but really not having a permanent home. However, all searches proved fruitless in my endeavor to find the chuck key

My searching went on for several minutes, then 20 minutes went by, then an hour and soon not only was I running out of places to look to find it, but I was also running out of patience in looking for it. My family well knows that when my patience gets tested, my temper certainly heats up.

My pressure valve for release of my rising temper has been to utter certain choice words, often words that as a kid I would have had my mouth washed out with soap for saying. With those words flying about, my wife would also try to help me by doing her best to keep me clam, while also looking around the work bench, the parts drawer, tool box and the like. All to no avail, with us eventually giving up as the chuck key was being elusive.

Needless to say, we were both unsuccessful in locating the chuck key and without it, the drill was not workable and as such the project I was going to try and accomplish would have to be put off until another time.

When I lose my patience with these 'inanimate objects', it takes a bit for me to calm down. Typically, some time would have to elapse before I would be calm enough to go onto another task or to just do something else.

"Patience means self-suffering", "To lose patience is to lose the battle" – Mahatma Ghandi

Side story: Patience has never been my strong suit. From a very early age I was always the antsy one. I was the one who couldn't wait to start something new – but no sooner had it been started I also wanted it to be finished. This had its advantage and disadvantage. For you see when it came to school work, I wanted to hurry and finish it and get onto playing. The same when it came to house chores too.

I would rather spend my time doing more enjoyable things and not a lot of the repetitive-mundane kinds of things. I enjoyed the newness of the task, but as soon as it became mundane, repetitive, or something got in the way of me finishing it, then that was a test of patience for me.

My family soon learned of my need to utter choice words to relieve the pressure I would endure during those frustrating times. The joke in our family soon became – Mom talking to the kids –'uh-oh dad's going to do some carpentry today, maybe we should go take a walk, or go out and do some shopping, or let's go visit so and so'. Anything to get out of the house and away from what might be my display of certain vocabulary.

For me, inanimate objects were my nemesis. I could not believe that it did not work correctly, or in the case of the chuck key, could not be found. As an example, my first job out of college was as a computer programmer. After I would create the code for the program, the next step was that I had to 'compile it'. This meant that I submitted the code file to an application that would check for syntax error such as missing semi-colons, uneven or not paired parenthesis, amongst other things that were of a more serious nature.

115

The process of compilation created an output file that I would look through to find the identified errors and then fix them. My problem with this process was that I thought that if the computer was smart enough to point out the syntax error, then it should have been smart enough to fix it and then just show me the result. But no, instead I had to go into the code and make the correction and then present it again for compilation. What a pain and as I thought, a big waste of time. Needless to say, I was at work and could not utter my normal vocabulary out loud – though I'm sure there were some choice words said under my breath.

Throughout working my day-job, my career as it were, my desire to get things done quickly was seen as both a positive and a challenge for those that worked with me. A positive being that whatever team of people I worked with, would most likely have their task(s) completed on time, but there was always a chance that I may rush it and make a mistake…which did happen, but not with a lot of frequency. The good news was that when a mistake was found, there was usually more than enough time to fix it without jeopardizing the schedule.

The good news for me was that later on in my career I moved into project management and in that I really found my career niche. I received many accolades for getting the projects done on time and within budget, but the bad news was that because of this I was given several projects to work on at the same time. As the old saying goes – if you want something done give it to a busy person. One thing for sure, I was never bored!!!

This chuck key really tested my patience, and of course my family – kids included, for they would hear the verbal barrage as I continued my searching for the elusive item. The parts drawer cabinet was my main storage for small items like the chuck key, and it was a simple and small cabinet that I had mounted to my work bench. There were 9 drawers in the cabinet; some held screws, others held washers, bolts, nails, drill bits, and on and on filling up the entirety of the 9 drawers. This is also where I would put my chuck key, and it really upset me that I could not find it there.

Over the next several days both my wife and I would look around the garage, rechecking all previously checked areas, including the parts drawer. By this time, it became a personal challenge to find it, a scavenger hunt of sorts, and no inanimate object was going to beat me.

Not being able to find this chuck key, I found myself asking my departed father – dad where do you think it could be? I might have also stated something like – dad I need some help finding the chuck key so if you could help me out here by pointing me in the right direction, I'd really appreciate it.

I continued my searching for a bit longer and without luck I found myself ending the search and calling it a day. A few more days had gone by and I really needed that chuck key as I not only needed to finish that first project but I now had another task where I also needed the drill, and not having the chuck key was the only obstacle standing in my way.

I decided to give the garage the once over one more time. First looking into the tool box, on the work bench and ending up looking back into the parts drawer. Opening up the parts drawers one by one and pushing aside the items in the drawer searching for the chuck key. Then after opening 3 or 4 drawers and not finding it, I opened up the next drawer, and I could not believe my eyes – there was the chuck key laying right up on top being the first thing I saw when I opened the drawer.

Still not believing what I was seeing, I grabbed the chuck key and went into the house to show my wife. Naturally she was happy for me while also asking me where I had found it. When telling her it was in the parts drawer, she responded with – "no really where was it". I reiterated that I found it in the parts drawer. Her mouth dropped open a bit as we both had searched that parts drawer not just once or twice but several times and the chuck key was not there.

At this time, I told her that I had asked for help from dad to show me where it was and that I believed he had helped me by doing what he had to – to put it in a place that he knew I would check. We both took comfort in that, and this was not going to be the last time we had such help from one of our departed loved ones.

For those who may be skeptical and say that it was our kids that had taken it and then put it back, at the time of this event our oldest was around 4 and the youngest was only 2, so I really do not think they had anything to do with this. And as for both my wife and I to be blind to finding the chuck key on our many earlier search attempts, I really do not think that's possible. By the way the total size of the container that held the parts drawers was about 9 or 10 inches wide, 7-8 inches deep, and 9 inches tall.

When I was young, we lived in house that my dad did a lot of major remodeling to. For some of this remodeling I assisted my dad by doing small things, as I was maybe 8 or 9. Some of the tasks might be handing my dad the tools he needed, or holding onto an end of a board that he needed to cut, or even sweeping up (my least favorite) the debris from the days' work. Whatever it was I got to see the progress, learning all the time, while spending time with my dad.

When my dad passed, my wife and I were on our honeymoon, and it was a real shock to the both of us. Talking to my dad at times like this helped me to keep in contact with him, as if he was still with us, while also helping to heal and accept his loss.

We accepted this final finding of the chuck key as having been a Sign, a visit from my dad. I am very grateful that he was still around helping, and I accept what this Sign showed me - that it was still possible to be asking my dad for help.

4.2 HIS HOUSE, THE LADY AND A QUESTION ANSWERED

Butch was always working, either at his job, or fixing up his house. He had a two (2) story Cape Cod style house that he had bought as somewhat of a fixer upper in a nice suburban neighborhood. A house he could call his own and turn into his castle over time, as both funding and help would allow, with help coming from family members or friends, and of course living close meant that I spent some time helping my brother.

His house needed work on electrical, plumbing, insulation, a new kitchen and eventually a new third bedroom in the upstairs of the house. The work was not in a major need right away, but it was needed to fulfill the vision Butch had for his house. Eventually the house would also need to be painted, and have a new furnace with A/C.

Besides Butch having a full-time job, he also helped me out in my sideline endeavor, a janitorial and maintenance business that I successfully ran for thirteen (13) years. This business was started on a shoestring and came about as a necessity for the office my wife was managing, who right before the holidays, had their maintenance company quit. My wife needed help to keep the office clean and the garbage emptied and I had agreed to help out. One day the neighboring business saw me cleaning and taking out the trash and asked if I had room in my schedule to clean their place, and of course I said yes, and with that my business was then official launched.

Butch had helped me for many of the thirteen years, and of course I paid him. The money he would then use for his needs including buying material for fixing up his house. Most of the stores and offices that we cleaned were in either mall and/or office building locations in the Monroe County area of NY. We would typically perform the cleaning duties over the weekend after the facilities were closed.

Saturday evenings around 9 pm I would arrive at Butch's house, grab a quick cup of coffee, and then off to the mall to perform our duties as soon as the store or office closed. During our cleaning time, we worked and chatted, and Butch would tell me of his plans for the house or we would comment on something from our jobs or whatever had happened in the news that day or week.

During the holidays the mall time schedule would change and the stores would stay open later which meant that we would have to start our cleaning later into the evening thus finishing into the wee hours of the morning. We sometimes extended that time as we would walk through the mall concourse and see all of the Christmas displays in their full glory, without being disturbed by the crowd of shoppers who had left upon the mall closing - a fun time that we looked forward to each year.

Year after year, Butch would work more on his house, and at times I would also help out. We took on many a task and a few he hired out to those more knowledgeable than we were. Over time Butch had managed to create a house that he was very proud of, and he continued to work on it until his untimely death.

When he passed, I became the executor of his estate, though he did not have much in the form of assets beyond his car, some retirement money, and of course his house. As executor I managed all of his financial arrangements, while my mom had taken care of his funeral arrangements.

Needless to say, one of the items I had to dispose of was his house. The only issue was the house was not in a finished state to put onto the housing market as there were a few projects in the middle of being worked on, while still others were on the 'To Do' list. This meant that I would need to arrange to have the house projects completed, doing most of the work myself, leaning upon other family members for assistants, calling in some favors, and also hiring other work out to the professionals.

Over the next several weeks we worked to fulfill Butch's vision for the house. One of the tasks was to design and complete the work on the upstairs bedroom, creating a master on-suite, complete with a sitting area, custom bath, and carpeted floors.

Another task needing completion was the enclosed front porch. While I hired out the work for the bathroom build, I completed the work on the front porch, doing some electrical and adding shiplap to the walls, then finally painting the walls and ceiling.

My wife is a great painter and she took on the painting of the living, dining room and the new master suite. Next, we tackled the outside work of landscaping adding greenery and mulch and painting of the garage. After all of the landscaping, building and painting was completed came the next step of staging the house for sale.

Every time I would go to his house in order to ready it for the sales market, I would ask aloud "**hey Butch do you like what we are doing, and are we are doing a good job**". On one visit I took a micro tape recorder with me. I did this hoping to perhaps capture an electronic voice phenomenon (EVP) of Butch's response as it really meant a lot to me that I completed his house in the manner that he would have approved. (What could I say, this was the same time frame that there were several Ghost related reality TV shows such as Ghost Hunters, and I was a fan.)

After the house work was completed, we immediately contacted a realtor that we had used before. When they came to view the house, the deal was signed to list it immediately. The realtor described the house as the quaint 'Pottery Barn' house and took several pictures for her listing. Needless to say, the listing did not last long on the market and within a few short weeks we were under contract for the sale.

When the sale was completed, I paid my last visit to the house to remove the staging and do a final clean and walk through. I was the last person to leave the house as I wanted to stay behind, and say my final goodbyes. This was an emotional time for me, but I did manage to once again ask Butch – "I truly hope we did you proud and that you liked and approved of the job we did completing the work on your house". And with that I closed the door for the last time, locking it behind me.

Over the next several months I often wondered what Butch would have thought of the house and the work we did to complete it for sale. There were times that my wife and I would be out running errands or taking a drive and we would cruise by his house just to see what the new owners might have been doing to his house.

The next year, during early spring time my daughter-in-law Julie was out running some errands with her children, our grandkids, all loaded up in the van. One of the errands took her down Mt Read Boulevard, past the corner street of Wildwood Drive, the street that led to my brother's house. Passing the street, she happened to notice an elderly woman attempting to leave the shopping plaza parking lot and trying to cross the busy intersection to the other side of the street.

Julie went a little further up the road, and as she tells us, something just told her to turn around and go back to see if she could assist that lady. She immediately turned around and ventured back to the woman, whom had not yet been able to make it across the street.

Pulling up alongside of the woman, she asked her if everything was OK, and did she need any help. The woman responded that her son's car was in the shopping plaza parking lot and it would not start, and so she was attempting to walk to their house which

124

was just down a bit on Wildwood Drive – the street my brother had lived on.

My daughter-in-law stated that she would be glad to drive her home and with the lady agreeing, Julie then helped the elderly woman up into the van and drove towards her house.

During the short drive they chatted briefly and the lady stated that she lived at 116 Wildwood Drive, and you might have guessed it already, that was my brother's old house. Julie, knowing this was my brother's house, explained to the woman that her husband's uncle had lived there and that he had recently passed away. She also mentioned that her uncle and father-in-law (me) worked on that house, fixing it up over the years until my brothers' untimely death.

The elderly woman was very understanding of the story, and after hearing about how the house was remodeled, the lady stated you tell your father-in-law that "they did a wonderful job" on fixing up the house. My daughter-in-law was not aware at the time that I had wondered about the work I had done at my brother's house and my question being – had we done a good job or not, and would my brother had been happy with it.

Later that day Julie recounted the story to my wife, telling her about the adventure and what the elderly woman had to say to her about the house. During the discussion my wife mentioned that I had always wondered about how Butch felt about the work we had done at his house, and that this encounter would give me the response I had been wanting.

When my wife related the story of Julie's adventure that day, goosebumps began to form on my arms. I needed to sit down and process all of this. Could it really be another Sign, a sign that my deceased brother Butch was communicating his appreciation for and approval of what we had done to finish the work at his house and ready it for sale? Perhaps, but it could also be a coincidence and maybe the elderly lady was just being very polite in her response.

However, for me I knew that the woman's comments and especially her word choice was just too close of a response for what I had been asking. I realized then that my quest of finding out if my brother had approved of the work done to his house was now complete, the conclusion to my wondering has been satisfied and with that my heart was full. And for me I continue to see and believe that this was a Sign that the Veil is thinner than we imagine.

4.3   THE AIRLINER MOTEL, AND A NEEDED PICTURE

Previously I had mentioned the lost chuck key to my drill. My searching for it endlessly, eventually becoming frustrated with the lack of finding it. How running out of options, I then asked aloud to my deceased dad for his help in locating the chuck key and the circumstances of its appearance.

126

Personally, I believe that the departed, for lack of any other way to describe it, are our angels that do indeed watch over us and are there to help us as best they can to guide and direct, and occasionally help us to find things that are lost. For me, this is the power and proof that there is an afterlife, and that once we have departed this mortal soil, we do not just cease to exist. This is my belief, but I understand that it may not be yours.

The chuck key incident has not been the only time that items have gone missing – only to turn up once we have exhausted all other avenues and turned to the ever watchful ones that have passed before us. I have called upon my deceased mom, dad and brother to help when I saw no other option, and especially if my actions having proved fruitless were beginning to frustrate me.

When writing my second book, *My Rosemount Mn. Memories – Teenage Years in My shoes*, I needed some pictures to compliment the writings. I knew we had some of the pictures, though my wife and I had remembered seeing them, we were unable to find them after many attempted searches.

While writing that book, the world was going through the Covid crisis, and for the most part we were pretty much confined to the house, venturing out only for the necessities where home delivery was not an option. During this so called **'two weeks to stop the curve'** house confinement – to pass the time, besides performing my writing, my wife and I were sorting through all of the family pictures that we had compiled over the many years of our marriage. We had taken over our dining room with the pictures spread out all over the dining table, onto the seats of chairs and continuing with picture boxes on the floor. Hundreds of pictures laid out before us with the goal of sorting, cataloguing and arranging them all into binders.

During this time, I had spent a considerable amount of effort online researching certain events for my book, talking with members at various historical societies, libraries, and the like. I was on a mission to find certain pictures and needed information in order to complete my stories and therefore my book, in the best possible manner commensurate with my efforts. For the most part I was having some success but I was still lacking in what was for me, finding of the really important pictures.

One of the pictures I wanted was that of the motel our family had first stayed in when we had moved to Minnesota, where my dad's company had transferred him. This motel was unique in appearance as it had an airplane mounted to the roof of the lobby of the motel.

The airplane had been placed on the roof of the motel by the motel owners, the LaMorias, as it was the airplane that they had used until it was decommissioned. Mounting the airplane to the roof had moved this motel into a local iconic state, a true tourist type landmark destination in order to view this plane.

The lobby of the Airliner Motel with airplane on its roof

The picture shown here is the picture that I knew we had in our collection; however, I was struggling to find it. Again, both my wife and I remember seeing it, but neither of us were successful in locating it.

Because of this motel's iconic status my search for this picture led me to query several local Minnesota Dakota County Historical Society historians. Those many contacts did state that they would love to have one of the motel's pictures with the airplane on the roof in their collections, but to date they have not been successful in doing so.

Striking out with that opportunity, I then turned my research to the town of Eagan where the motel resided and began searching their local government website. Again, however, I was met with the same response, no pictures, although the searching did lead me to some other historical documents about the motel such as building permits and the like.

My searching would also involve trying to find the LaMorias –
hoping that they may have some of the pictures of their time
owning the motel. Unfortunately, I had found that the LaMorias
had passed away, and that their only living relative was a sister
who was elderly. My attempts to contact her were not successful
and as such I was still at a loss of finding what I considered to be
a very needed picture to complete the book.

Not having any success, and having once again rechecked all of
our pictures that lay sprawled out on the dining room table, I felt I
needed some additional help, maybe some spiritual guidance
you might say. It was at this point I called upon my departed
family members to assist here by pointing me in the direction of
where that picture may indeed be hiding. And with that thought
in mind I stated the following out loud, "Mom, Dad, Butch if you
can help find the picture and put it in a prominent spot that I can
find it, or in some way point me in the direction of the picture it
would be greatly appreciated".

I continued my search confident that I might locate it – but again
my efforts were met with disappointment. Repeatedly my wife
and I looked for that picture, and still we came up empty-handed.
I was beginning to wonder if we would ever find it.

But that was not the only picture that I needed, I also wanted a
picture of the shopping plaza in Apple Valley, Minnesota showing
the grocery store that I and many of my high school friends
worked at – Penny's Supermarket. And to top it off there was a

question being asked on social media regarding the official name of that shopping plaza, with many guesses having been offered.

One day, for some unknown reason, I felt an overwhelming need to check some of my brother Butch's photo albums that I had acquired upon his passing. My brother's hobby was photography and he was pretty good at it. His albums were not included with the pictures on the dining room table, and in fact I had not looked through them at all as I had a really hard time emotionally looking through any of his photos and other personal items since his passing some eleven (11) years earlier. Instead, these items were kept in a covered tote tucked away in the far back corner of my clothes closet.

Maybe now was the time that I needed to come to terms with his death and to begin looking at his passing as a part of life, to relish in his memory and further my own healing by enjoying the many photos that he made possible through his love of photography.

I cannot really express as to why I felt I had to do this now, but whatever the reason I knew that I had to do it, almost like I was being directed to do so. Gathering the tote from the closet and taking out the photo albums, I began to page through them, enjoying the pictures, reminiscing about the past and the good times, however, still no picture of the motel with the airplane.

Continuing my review of the album, page by page, I was enjoying the further trip down memory lane. Though my brother had never married, there were pictures in the album of a trip he took with a girlfriend he was seeing at the time, a trip to Minnesota, the state where the girl's family was living.

Turning the album pages, I was reminded of my time living in Minnesota and some of the sites there, and as I turned page by page there were many pictures showing the areas that I had once traveled. Then as I ventured further into the album pages, I came upon a page that had a few pictures on it. And all of a sudden there it was in all its glory – the picture of the old shopping plaza, the plaza with the super market I and my friends worked at in the 1970's.

Wow, wow, wow I could not believe that I finally found a photo of that plaza, and that my brother had it in his collection all this time. Many memories had come back to me upon seeing this picture. And oh yeah, by the way, there in the picture, was the plaza entrance sign with the plaza name on it. What a find!

Though I couldn't help think that maybe I was somehow directed to this album and this picture. Why now, at this time did I want to finally venture into my brothers' belongings – belongings that have been buried in the back corner of my closet, and up till now I did not want to look at it. I did ask my departed family members for help, and perhaps I was being guided by my brother.

When I thought about how I was going to use the picture in my book, I realized that I also needed to do a couple of other things with the picture. First, I scanned the photo into my computer, and began to format the picture for use. Next, I cropped it and enhanced the photo – sharpening it for greater clarity. Then I copied the newly formatted picture into an email and sent it to two good friends of mine who also worked with me at the super market. Following that I went onto social media, found the inquiry about the plaza name and uploaded my picture with a message about what the plaza name was – with the picture plainly showing the plaza entrance sign. Finally, I put a copy of the picture into a page of my book, a page that had information about my working at the plaza super market with my friends.

Feeling good by my actions and with one problem solved, I returned to my efforts of finding the picture of the motel with the airplane on the roof. Heading back into the dining room I once again looked through the many photos that lay upon the dining room table. Still coming up empty handed I decided to once again reiterate my ask to mom, dad and Butch for their help, hoping that one more time perhaps they could lead me to success in the finding of that picture.

My wife and I continued our searching for the elusive picture of the motel with the airplane on its roof. We searched again through all of the pictures on the dining room table, looking through Butch's picture albums, and any other place we could think of. I also continued my inquiries on social media, and even contacted a local VFW that had been located down the street from the motel, but had moved to a new location. Though the VFW member I spoke with was able to recall the motel and the plane on its roof, unfortunately he could not help me in locating a picture of it.

All of our searching was proving fruitless, and to be honest I was getting pretty discouraged that the picture we knew we once had, the picture of that iconic motel was now maybe lost forever.

It had been a few days since I had last asked my departed family members for help, and a few days since we last encircled the dining room table immersing ourselves in the many photos collected there. Again, for some unknown reason I said aloud that "I know we have that picture", and with that I decided to go look again around the dining room table.

Once more I found myself looking around the table at photos of family, of places and events I took part in, photos of past loved ones and those of friends. I could not help but to reminisce of a by-gone time. Some of the pictures portraying a simpler time, some of great events and adventures our family have enjoyed, and some more solemn pictures of those that have passed.

Walking around the end of the dining table I looked at the multi-picture frame that had many family pics in it. Pictures of family both present and passed, only this time something looked different and it caught my eye. During prior investigations I had not noticed that the glass from the picture frame was sitting on top of the frame and not enclosed within the frame. I don't recall noticing this before – perhaps I was blind to it, but given the many times both my wife and I had looked at those pictures you would have thought we would have remembered seeing that.

As I examined the frame further, I also noticed that there in the corner of the frame was a small stack of pictures sandwiched between the glass on top of the frame, and the framed pictures. This is not something I could have missed, not something my wife would have missed either, but there it was. The pictures were stacked up on top of each other, about eight (8) pictures in total.

Upon seeing those pictures, I carefully removed the glass that and set it aside. Taking the stack of photos out of the frame I began thumbing my way through them. Then all of a sudden like a flash of lighting, there it was, in all its splendor and glory – the picture of the motel with the airplane on the roof. Was this really real, and how did we not see this stack of pictures on our many, many, many searches?

I had to take a minute to fully grasp what I was seeing, just to make sure I was awake and not hallucinating. I had feelings of joy, and giddy jubilance, almost childlike excitement – not unlike that of a child waking up on Christmas morning.

What follows is the type of multi picture frame that I have referenced. This picture shows the frame with the glass inside the frame and the pictures covered by the glass. When I found the stack of pictures, the glass was sitting on top of the frame. The interesting part for my wife and I was that first we had not

135

seen the stack of pictures upon our searching, and secondly, we
had not remembered at all that the glass was sitting on top of the
frame.

Immediately I put the other pictures back onto the frame, and
took the picture of the motel to show my wife. When I showed
her, the look on her face was, to say the least, showing both the
thrill and shock at the discovery. We both just looked at each
other with a bit of a half smirk-smile on our faces, just enough for
each of us to acknowledge that this was yet another Sign; and
that having asked our departed for assistance, they had listened
and helped by working their magic once more.

Relieved that my search was over, I could now get back to
finishing the writing of my book, and it would now be able to be
completed with the placement of the final picture which would be
prominently displayed within the book, and also adding that
picture to the books' front cover.

Over the next couple weeks, I finished writing the book readying it for the printers. All was finally in order and the goals for this second book were now completed. Additionally, I contacted the several historical societies alerting them of my find and providing them with an online copy of the photo for their archives. And to complete the sharing of the picture, I emailed a copy of the picture to the VFW acquaintance I had spoken with as he was also an avid plane enthusiast.

I have to ask the questions – was the finding of the picture merely a matter of my persistence of searching through the dining room table of pictures we had laid out there, searching until my eyes fixed upon the stack of pictures that contained it? Could my wife and I both, through our many searches of the pictures that lay upon the dining table, been blind to the picture frame glass and the stack of pictures beneath it – well I guess it's possible, though some how I feel it very unlikely.

My conclusion is that after my continued searching, and disappointment, and my repeated asks of my departed family to help me, to either direct me to or in some way leave the picture in a place that I could find it, that they were finally able to assist me on my quest. I truly have to accept that either that had happened or that both my wife and I have immediate need of an optometrist's services.

"Ask, and it shall be given you; seek, and ye shall find; knock, and it shall be opened unto you:" Matthew 7:7 (KJV)

Though this is not an exactly right quote to use here – from a biblical perspective that is – I felt it represented what I believe when I decide to interact with the departed. Once again tis has shown me that indeed the Veil is thinner than we imagine!

4.4   A GRIEVING WIFE AND A WAYWARD BALLOON

Over the years we have had numerous occasions where we would often ponder the reason(s) of what we were experiencing often wondering and metaphorically speaking – was it the breeze or was it something else.

Sharon's mom, Char, lived well into her 80's. The last few years of her life she was living not far from our house in an adult care facility. Char's health had been deteriorating over the years to the point that she could no longer physically care for herself, though her mental faculties were still intact. And my wife would help care for her mom visiting almost daily, spending time with her and bringing the great-grandkids by for visits.

Throughout the year when family events and holidays would come about, Sharon would pick her mom up from the facility and bring her to our house for the day. We would spend time with her telling stories, laughing and just enjoying the day. And as was accustomed we would enjoy a small glass of wine together. Char had always looked forward to this time, as did we all.

This routine went on for some time until we got the call that Char had fallen at the facility. We immediately went to the residency

138

and checked in on her. Sharon had been a strong advocate for her mom's health care and decided, due to circumstances, to stay overnight with Char, and I headed back home.

Over the next few weeks, we could see that Char was not getting any better, and it was soon thereafter that her mom passed as a result of complications from the fall. Though we had expected this, it was still a bit of a shock, and very upsetting.

Both of Sharon's parents were now deceased and so was my dad. The only living parent now was my mom, and though we had no way of knowing at the time, my mom would only live another six (6) months before she too would pass due to complications from a fall.

Sharon was depressed, one of the five signs of grieving after a loved one has passed. Over the next several days and weeks she would often sit outside under the covered patio. This was the same place that her mom and her would sit when her mom was visiting, weather permitting, and they would chat about many things. They loved to chat about gardening, grandkids, and to tell stories from her and her mom's life. Occasionally I would bring out a small glass of wine, which would make her mom light up a bit, after all she enjoyed a drink from time to time, and there was no drinking at her care facility.

With her mom's passing, Sharon would sit there all alone thinking about her mom, and of course (knowing my wife) she would also think about if there was anything else she may have been able to do to have prolonged her mom's life. As we all do perhaps, doubts of our own inadequacies permeating our thoughts as we contemplate theirs and our immortality. At times Sharon would speak to her mom, out loud, as though she was still sitting there with her, often just random thoughts, thoughts of kindness and love, with the occasional asking that if her mom could hear her to please in some way to let her know.

Sharon was grieving, and try as I might, there was nothing I could say to take away the pain and the tears, but I could be there with a gentle smile, a warm embrace, and at times a shoulder to cry upon. Though it was hard, Sharon was going through some of the more difficult stages of grief as she had not yet reached the final step of acceptance.

Over our years together, Sharon and I have received Signs and would always contemplate their meaning, at times just marveling at the apparent timing of the receipt of the sign. And this next sign was no different in its forthcoming.

Sharon's mom had passed on a Tuesday, and that following Sunday Sharon sat outside under the covered patio, and spoke aloud to her mom asking for a sign that her mom was still with her. That following Monday Sharon was moving about inside the house doing some daily chores when through the kitchen window something from outside caught her eye attention. Sharon watched as an object, a bit shiny in the suns light, was flittering down from the sky and was starting to become viewable at the top of the tree line in our backyard.

Continuing to watch the object on its path, ever downward and heading towards our patio area, Sharon could begin to see the object more clearly as it was taking shape and coming more into focus. Slowly drifting downward and eventually coming to rest in a chair beneath the covered patio. The object that now sat upon the chair, as if looking towards the window Sharon was peering out through, was a rosy-pink mylar balloon. This balloon was now resting in the chair where Sharon's mom would sit when the two of them were outside talking under the covered patio.

Was this the Sign Sharon had been seeking, the one that was letting Sharon know that her mom was still here, or was this just some random balloon that had drifted away from a party, flew over wooded area, proceeding through our backyard, flying under the covered patio roof and just happen to come to rest in the chair underneath the covered patio where Sharon's mom would sit?

Sharon's eyes widened and mouth opened as she saw the balloon resting in what she called – her mom's chair. Carefully we rationalized the balloon and its meaning, and of course we both now believed that this was indeed another Sign. But why rosy pink in color, I mean typically we associate pink with a girl color, but could it be much more, perhaps a deeper meaning?

From a truly psychological perspective there are a lot of associations made to the color pink. Some of them are that the color pink represents passion, kindness, and understanding; the

141

color pink embodies all that is good in the world. As an exceedingly approachable color, pink doesn't intimidate or threaten. Instead, it offers the opposite effect and those who encounter this shade are often overcome with unbridled joy. The color pink provides warmth and comfort and when we see the color pink, it inspires us to cling to hope. There's no obstacle too big for pink to overcome, and as for rosy pink, the color of that balloon, that is the universal color of love.

Sharon truly believed that her mom was indeed sending her a message – a message of hope and love as only a mother can. This message is what Sharon really needed at that time, a message that would enable her to begin moving into the acceptance stage of grieving. This acceptance part does not happen overnight but it is a process that must have a beginning and I believe that the balloon on that day – for Sharon – was the trigger for the acceptance process to begin.

Sharon has kept that balloon in her closet and sees it every day, first thing in the morning as she is getting ready to take on the day's activity, a reminder that life is precious and that love is everlasting. We both realize that this was indeed a Sign from her departed mom. A Sign that the Veil is definitely thinner than we imagine.

'Love bears all things, believes all things, hopes all things endures all things. Love never ends.' 1 Corinthians 13:7-8

5 GROUPING FIVE: ANIMALS AND NUMBERS

Have you had animals or insects suddenly come to you in ways that are not common? For example, having a bird fly up to you and land on your hand, or a butterfly make a mid-air turn and fly towards you and land on you. Have you repeatedly seen the same set of numbers (such as 1234) show up? For example, you receive a sales receipt and the total was $ 12.34, or you happen to glance at a clock and the time is 12:34, or in any other way see the same set of numbers over and over again?

Within this section will be stories that specifically deal with Signs delivered by nature's animals, or by way of seeing the same random set of numbers over and over. Not all of these signs are necessarily understood upon receipt and sometimes the sign may be very personal and only understood by the recipient.

5.1 A HUMMINGBIRD AND A BUTTERFLY

We have discussed various types of Signs that I and others have experienced, and so far, they have been received through various ways. Some occurrences, such as lost items all of a sudden showing up after exhaustive searches were made, some Signs being delivered via an inanimate object such as the battery-operated device that all of a sudden started on its own. And then there were the more divine and miraculous ones too.

But the animal world has not yet been explored and I believe too, that they have sent me a sign, one I still ponder to this day, but one that I felt very comforted by.

I have previously mentioned that there is a belief that seeing a red cardinal after the loss of a loved one symbolizes a visit from the other side, a message that the soul of the deceased person is still with you and that you're not alone in this world. The red cardinal is said to symbolize eternal flame and immortality, and its feathers are also said to symbolize the blood of Christ.

Personally, after all of these experiences, I truly believe that our departed loved ones are trying to communicate with us and they're finding ways to do so. The red cardinal, for example, is one of the ways that they are doing it.

Our departed are attempting to communicate with us and deliver messages that they want to help us with our grieving process, or they're trying to tell us their souls are still with us and they will be there forever. Maybe they want to say that our life is a part of a bigger plan and that life continues after death, just differently.

Many Native Americans tribes respected animals, and they had the deepest respect for birds, especially for the red cardinal. They believed that red cardinals are messengers of the departed. They worshiped this colorful bird and explained that seeing a red cardinal after someone's death was an encounter with souls of the deceased warriors who had fallen in recent battles. They used the red cardinal's feathers as a lucky charm believing that the feathers would protect them in following wars.

From a Christian viewpoint the cardinal is a symbol of Christ's blood. It represents reincarnation and eternal love. A red cardinal is the most common bird that is mentioned together with angels, and is thought to be a voice sent from Heaven, and a cardinal's red color indicates that it has been touched by the divine flame.

Therefore, it's easy to see that there is a connection made that seeing a red cardinal upon someone's death is considered to be a good sign, one that you can take comfort in. But what about seeing a hummingbird or a butterfly, is that also relatable to the spiritual world, well turns out that it is and that is where my next Sign story will take us.

Our house has a three car garage. Frequently the garage doors are opened if we are outside working in the yard, or visiting with the neighbors, etc... One day we were outside working when my wife calls me to come to the garage. Upon arrival I see her pointing to the ceiling. Looking upward at the ceiling I observe that a hummingbird has perched itself upon the wire leading to the garage door opener.

Though surprised by this at first, I knew that we had to find a way to gracefully extricate this bird from the garage without harming it. Looking around the garage for some inspiration as to how best to remove the bird, I grabbed a nearby broom and tried to shoo him off the wire and into the outside area. After a few attempts at doing this, I realized that this bird was not willing to move on, so I had to come up with another plan of attack.

My immediate thought was that if I could get the bird to perch on the broom bristle, perhaps I could walk him outside and then release him into the open yard. I proceeded to do this by gently raising the broom, bristle side up, bringing it ever closer to the bird. After a couple attempts the bird then stepped onto the bristles. Feeling success I brought him outside, to which he then immediately flew back inside of the garage.

Now it was time to get really serious as I was determined to free this bird from my garage, unharmed, and released back into the wild from which he came. I again raised the broom, bristle side up towards the bird. The bird again, stepped onto the bristles. This time though, I lowered the broom just until the top of the bristles were level with my chin.

The hummingbird and I were now looking eye-to-eye. We paused there for a moment just looking at each other. Slowly I began to raise my hand, my index finger extended outwards, up along the side of the bristles until my finger was right underneath the birds' feet. Ever so slowly I raised my finger and in doing so I forced the bird to let go of the bristles and step onto my finger. Success, as the bird was now using my finger as a perch. My thought was to walk the bird outside of the garage and with a slight flick of my finger release him back into the wide-open outdoors.

Slowly I walked with the bird, heading for the outside. Once there I walked another 10 yards or so away from the garage, the hummingbird still perched upon my finger.

Stopping in the driveway, I stood still and just admired that the bird was still with me, and once more we locked eyes. We stood there looking at each other for what seemed like several minutes, but I'm sure it was just mere seconds. Both of us calm in our nature, almost like we were connected beyond just being species comingling on planet Earth. Something more was happening, but I lack the words to describe the feeling at that moment. Then in a blink of an eye the hummingbird flew off into the trees.

What had I just experienced? I had to think about this one. Was there something more to this encounter – was it more than just a bird trapped in my garage, a garage with three doors, all of them open. I went back to my chores, but all the while thinking about what had happened.

Later on, upon researching the meaning of hummingbirds, I found it stated that angels will often use animals as messengers, especially birds as they can travel great distances. There is so much written about the visitation by a hummingbird that it has me really wondering the meaning of and the message from my own experience.

The very next day my wife and I were relaxing on our back deck, just enjoying the sounds of nature, comforted with the fact that the chores were done and we were now just sitting content with each other's company. Then, as if out of nowhere, a butterfly made its appearance and fluttered by us. However, as we sat in our chairs watching it fly by, that butterfly then did a complete turnaround in mid-air, and flew back towards us.

Without further fanfare it headed directly to me and landed upon my shoulder. My wife and I were stunned a bit at first, but then we began looking at each other. Both of us were simultaneously thinking and perhaps knowing too that this was not just happenstance, that this was yet perhaps another Sign.

I remember joking at first that the hummingbird must have told his nature buddies that I was one of the good guys, and that the butterfly was just here to confirm that. But there we sat, further relaxing with this butterfly continuing to rest upon my shoulder.

For what was probably the next 10 minutes the three of us sat there, my wife and I chatting softly as we both watched this butterfly perched upon my shoulder – every once in a while, flapping his wings. Then as if by cue, he flapped his wings once again and flew off circling us while we sat there watching his movements. Soon he flew off into the yard and out of sight.

After this my wife and I discussed what had happened in the last two days. Why did the bird and the butterfly stay with me so long? I even joked about perhaps becoming Dr. Dolittle. Both of us now feeling curious and perhaps a bit befuddled at how the

148

past two days' events had unfolded. (By the way it's been a few years and this type of event has not happened since that time.)

Wanting to know more and especially wanting to understand how these two creatures are maybe connected and what they may symbolize, I turned to the internet and began my research.

Butterflies have long been associated with being messengers of departed souls. This belief is held within many cultures and so much so that there is also special meaning given to the delivered message depending upon what color the butterfly wings are.

Personally, I have to admit that some of this maybe mere coincidence, but I cannot yet explain why the butterfly had chosen to turn around in midflight, head towards me and land on my shoulder. This butterfly was a Monarch which are fairly prevalent in north America. We typically see them in our yard fluttering around but when we have attempted to get close to them, they usually fly off.

Thinking about it for a while, I wondered if the two occurrences were somehow connected. One of my research discoveries was that your past loved one is now pure energy. They are said to be able to channel this energy into an insect or animal and for a brief period of time bring you a sign that their spirit lives on.

> **They may appear to you in this way as a butterfly**, *dove, rabbit, dragonfly, or any other number of insects or animals... When this happens, the animal or insect*

149

will **usually do something that is out of character** that catches *your attention*. **They may land on your hand**, come into your home, or appear closely, **right in front of you as if they are communicating**.

I copied the above paragraph from an article titled: ***Signs from Heaven ... 9 Signs from Deceased Loved Ones, written by*** Tyra Love, Updated August 23, 2022. Coincidently I noticed too the words Signs in the title of the article, as also in the title of my book. Highlighting text from the copied paragraph I can see that perhaps my suspicions that there was something more to the butterfly visit might just be so.

What about the experience with the hummingbird? Again, from my internet searching I found an article title: ***Visited by a Hummingbird? What Does It Mean Spiritually?*** by Rose Putnam. This article describes from a spiritual perspective the meaning of seeing a hummingbird and it further describes the symbolism that cultures have placed upon them. The article stated that:

> '...*throughout history, hummingbirds have held spiritual significance. In Native American animism* (the belief that all creatures possess a spiritual essence), *hummingbirds were believed to be spiritual helpers and lightworkers. Seeing a hummingbird represented peace, love, and harmony. They were always drawn as a symbol in a pair, which was to depict the energy of union, devotion, domestic harmony, and honoring the life cycles.*

The Aztecs believed that hummingbirds had a strong connection to their ancestors, and when a hummingbird would appear it was a visitation from loved ones who have passed on. They were also seen as messengers from the gods.

While hummingbirds are small, they are confident, aggressive, and aren't afraid to defend their territory. As such, they represent a new layer of confidence that comes from knowing that you are protected and guided by Divine and pure loving energy. This new connection to self makes you stand up for your values and push energies away that don't align with your highest essence.

Being visited by a hummingbird should give you a renewed sense of hope and faith, finally seeing the bigger picture, knowing that all your grief is leading you towards a higher path. The hummingbird is letting you know that everything has happened for a reason.'

There is a lot of information written about the spiritual nature of hummingbirds and their visitation upon you. There is meaning given to not only the visit itself, but also the time of the visit – be it after a loved one's death, during a time of confusion, thinking about of a change in life – or being on the right path.

Suzanne Somers died October 15, 2023. Her husband Alan Hamel said recently *in the article: Unexplained Things Have Been Happening Since Her Death,* by Katie Jerkovich, (Jan 16, 2024 DailyWire.com) – that he has experienced many strange events since Suzanne's death, events that have now made him a believer in the after-life.

In the article he stated: "A hummingbird flew into our house and made the rounds in the kitchen, and the living room and the dining room,". He added that the bird "hovered" in front of a framed photo of he and Suzanne, and "landed on top and stayed there."

From all of the reading I have done, there is the constant mentioning of the Life Force and how the hummingbird is attracted to this life force energy. There is much meaning given to the spirituality of the hummingbird just as there is to the butterfly. Some of the meanings can be assigned by the different colors of the bird, the birds feathers (especially held in high esteem by native American cultures) - and also if it's a baby hummingbird.

Perhaps all of this is nothing more than superstition, old wife's tales as it were, even pure fantasy or just plain nonsense. Whatever it may be, real or fantasized, I cannot deny that I felt something unusual on the days that I had the encounters with the hummingbird and the butterfly.

And the forever analyst in me has to challenge myself to dig deeper, to discover if there was something more than just the experience of these two events. What are the odds of these events occurring, why did they occur when they did and what is the message I should take from their occurrence. These are the things that make me go Hmmm!

For as Socrates has stated… *"The unexamined life is not worth living."*

5.2   NUMERICAL SIGNS

Everyone would love to have the winning lottery numbers, especially when the prize is several hundred million dollars. The thought of what and how it would change your life, how you might be able to help others with their lives are often what the mind is occupied with, especially during those times of extreme jackpots! And even though as the saying goes – 'you need to be in it to win it', we all know that our odds of winning are usually several million to one, and not at all in our favor!

Playing the lottery can be fun indeed, and the occasional few dollars of winning keeps your interest in the buying of more tickets. For me, I have not been that lucky at all in playing, but I still keep hoping, as millions of others do, that one day it just might pay off in a big way.

Side Story: I have a buddy Joel, whose wife did win one million dollars in a scratch off lottery game. But that was not the first time she had won something big. Joel has told me that his wife spends a healthy amount weekly on scratch off lottery tickets. She then takes them to her living room to 'play them' by scratching them off one at a time.

Joel's wife has won not just the one million, but several other times winning $5, $10, $100, $10,000 or more. I was visiting them one day and she had a bunch of tickets, taking them to the living room to scratch off. All of a sudden, we heard her yell in excitement as she had just had another winning ticket, and this time it was for $15,000. I saw the ticket and still could not believe it. All I could think was good for her and boy is she lucky.

By the way, the living room where she would always sit to scratch off these tickets, I am not kidding when I tell you this, the living room was covered with angel statues. Porcelain, wood, metal, all depicting angels. I commented to Joel about this and all he said was that is the only place his wife will scratch off those lottery tickets.

Coincidence, perhaps, but what can I say other than maybe I should go purchase some angel statues!

There was another case of a Sign that culminated with the purchase of a lottery ticket that paid off big for one very lucky woman. Here is her story.

A Washington woman, revealed to be the winner of a record Powerball jackpot, claims she purchased her ticket after seeing a "sign" at a grocery store.

Becky Bell, of Auburn, stopped into her local Fred Meyer on Feb. 5 to purchase $20 worth of lottery tickets. She usually buys the same tickets every week, but after catching a glimpse of the then-estimated jackpot amount on a lottery vending machine — $747 million — she knew she had to shell out an extra few bucks for an additional Powerball ticket, according to a press release from the Washington Lottery.

Bell, as it just so happens, has worked for Boeing for the last 36 years. And just days before she walked into that supermarket, Boeing delivered the company's very last 747 aircraft, to instead focus production on newer, more fuel-efficient planes.

"That's when it hit me … I had to buy one more ticket," Bell told the Washington Lottery.

Bell checked her ticket the morning after the Feb. 6 drawing and learned she had won the $754,550,826 grand prize, which is the fifth-largest Powerball jackpot in the history of the game. Still somewhat unbelieving what was happening, she then woke up her children to verify what she was seeing.

"I've never won more than $20 in my life, so you can imagine my shock when I realized what had just happened," Bell said.

Speaking later with lottery officials, Bell chalked up her win to more than just a cosmic coincidence. "I told you it was a Sign," Bell said.

Numerical coincidence prompted $754M Powerball winner to buy ticket: 'It was a sign' | RochesterFirst

(https://www.rochesterfirst.com/news/national-news/numerical-coincidence-prompted-754m-powerball-winner-to-buy-ticket-it-was-a-sign/?utm_source=facebook.com&utm_medium=referral&utm_campaign=socialflow&fbclid=IwAR0f3cwVLzwEvUXCyPF6H0mPp1HZr-wAo_sl_EyC3_aUQ2KeM7h5PTI_Fpw)

Unbelievable too is the fact that this sign just happened to be in a store in Washington State. The same state where Boeing has its factory that manufactured the 747 airplane! Coincidence perhaps or maybe as Ms. Bell says **"I told you it was a Sign"**.

Now I am not at all implying that you can win the lottery, and in fact I believe that the Cosmos, angels, etc. are not going to send you a sign for you to win the lottery. Personally, I do not think that it works that way. However, I believe the point of the story is that one must be ever vigilant to see and accept Signs, that they are indeed happening around us.

Proving my point that the Cosmos is not going to supply you with the numbers for winning the lottery, I recall my son-in-law Jason's story. As I shared in another chapter about my grandkids and the Red Bird candy that their other grandmother would give to them, well that grandmother was Jason's mom.

Not long after Jason's mom's passing, Jason was missing his mom terribly, and at times would talk out loud to her as if she was in the room. At this point, Jason, having the tasks of taking care of his family, now also had an added task of helping his dad manage some of his day to day affairs. With the mounting pressure of the additional work on top of Jason's already packed schedule, Jason once again found himself turning to his mom and asking for some help.

Jason, as he was heard asking out loud – mom if you are here with us, can you give me some help and/or guidance in winning the lottery? Well, nothing more was said about that until Jason, having just eaten Chinese food, was now cracking open the fortune cookie and retrieving his fortune. Upon reading the fortune – Jason received his answer. The fortune read 'if your desires are not extravagant, they will be granted'.

With that fortune being read, Jason understood that he should not ask for such extravagance. And for me upon hearing this story I too understood that the afterlife is not here to grant our wishes, but that they are definitely here and listening.

157

> # If your desires are not extravagant they will be granted.

Copy of the Fortune from the Cookie

Numbers have always been important for me. I took to the subject of math right away as it was logical, had a right answer, and you were able in many cases to cross check the result to verify that it was the right answer. Often, I could visualize the numbers in my head with the answer there – in picture format!

However, now I have come to view numbers a bit more cautiously, perhaps with more of an eye, or thought, as to their meaning. Pythagoras, in 500 B.C., suggested that everything can be stated in terms of numbers, giving rise to numerology. Modern mathematicians appear to be in agreement.

What do I mean by all of this? Well, let me first pose a question to you. **Have you seen the same set of numbers showing up at different times, but always the same ones?** Have they just randomly shown up let's say while watching TV, looking at a wall clock, getting some mail from a certain address, or just checking out at a store and there is that set of numbers as the total on the receipt? Well, if you have, you are certainly not alone. Coincidence, perhaps, but maybe this is yet another Sign, and one that you might want to pay attention to.

158

In Douglas Adams' *The Hitchhiker's Guide to the Galaxy*, 42 is the number from which all meaning ("the meaning of life, the universe, and everything") can be derived. In reality there is actually quite a few references to the number 42, from Buddhism to Catholicism, even to physics, the number 42 can be seen.

For example:

- In ancient Egyptian mythology, during the judgment of souls, the dead had to declare before 42 judges that they had not committed any of 42 sins.

- The marathon distance of 42.195 kilometers corresponds to the legend of how far the ancient Greek messenger Pheidippides traveled between Marathon and Athens to announce victory over the Persians in 490 B.C. (The fact that the kilometer had not yet been defined at that time only makes the connection all the more astonishing.)

- Ancient Tibet had 42 rulers. Nyatri Tsenpo, who reigned around 127 B.C., was the first. And Langdarma, who ruled from 836 to 842 A.D. (i.e., the 42nd year of the ninth century), was the last.

- The Gutenberg Bible, the first book printed in Europe, has 42 lines of text per column and is also called the "Forty-Two-Line Bible."

For me however I have a different set of numbers – numbers that I have seen often and these occurrences have me wondering as to why I am seeing them, is it another Sign and does it have any significant meaning behind it.

The numbers I have repeatedly seen have been 123 and 1234. Why these sets of numbers and why am I seeing them, and on occasion several times a day.

For example, at my age I may have to get up in the middle of the night to use the bathroom. When I get up and look at the clock there is the time 1:23. When I am driving in my car and look at the clock – there it is again 12:34 or 1:23. I was recently checking out at a store and there it was again those number $12.34 on the receipt.

I have a cardiologist appointment once a year, and in between the appointments I record my blood pressure, weight, and exercise numbers onto a spreadsheet. The spreadsheet has many tabs, each representing the month of the year that the results are recorded for. At the end of each month the numbers are averaged and summarized. For this last month the average of all my Systolic numbers was, you guessed it – 123.

These are not just recent occurrences as I have seen them for many years. I took a trip to Florida a few years ago, to visit my good friends there, and usually while I am on vacation, I typically do not check my watch. While we were at their home, my buddy says its 12:34 and we should get ready to go.

Often, I have seen this sequence of numbers show up, and recently I have also been seeing the number 222; again, be it with time, or reading, or just as a bill. I have seen these numbers so many times that they cannot all be coincidence.

Once again, the forever analyst in me is curious – what is causing them to be present in my life more so than other numbers? With this curiosity I began to look at the meaning of the numbers 123, 1234 and 222. And this curiosity took me down a path of discovery to what are called '**Angel Numbers**'.

Now I know what you may be thinking – this guy is certifiable, he's crazy. Well, I can't blame you as there are times that I too think all of this stuff is crazy, but then again, I cannot ignore the coincidence of seeing the same numbers repeatedly showing up out of the blue. And just like the hummingbird and butterfly, I know I have to do my research and try to understand why.

Beginning the research was not really easy as I was not sure where to start, so I decided to do an online search of the meaning of seeing the numbers 1234, or 123. That is when the results showed clearly that there was something to this and they were called Angel Numbers. The analyst in me said that I needed to dig deeper and that just because angel numbers were amongst the first results does not mean that is all I need to know.

My continued research took me down a path of religious significant of the numbers, the psychological meaning of the numbers, and on and on – but always with the theme of angel numbers. No matter how many 'MORE' buttons I hit at the bottom of the results list, I kept seeing it over and over and over again – angel Numbers!

How come if the internet search results are showing so many entries for angel numbers, why have I not heard much about them before? I'm entering interesting territory here as I am not what you would call a church going religious person. In fact, I have a hard time with today's church services with all the guitars and drums, people dressed in jeans and sweats; it appears to me to be more of a rock concert than a sermon.

Being raised a Methodist, I attended church services, Sunday School and the like. There was a choir, an organist, and a minister that pounded the podium each Sunday while preaching from the Bible. We went to church services each week, that is until there was a bit of a falling out between my parents and the church minister. I'm not sure what it was all about but that was pretty much the end of my formalized religious teachings.

Though I am a believer in God, and I have my own personal chats with the all-mighty, I still have questions regarding how the appointed religious teachers have related God's message over time. How is it that when you look at the King James Bible there are 50+ books, the Catholic Bible has 70+ books and the Ethiopian Bible has over 80 books. Would you not think that if we were all teaching the same gospel, the same word of God, that all of them would be the same in number of books?

When conducting an internet search on the number of books in the King James Bible for example, the search results do not even match as to the number of books – as I have found anywhere from 44 books to 66 books to 80 books as listed for being in the King James Bible. But I am not getting into a biblical discussion here as I am sorely lacking in any in-depth biblical knowledge to discuss any of it in great detail.

Getting back to angel numbers, I am intrigued by the concept of numbers that are said to have spiritual significance. I am sort of thinking of this in the same vein as I think of horoscopes, Chinese fortune cookies, superstitions, and things that go bump in the night. But I cannot find any valid rational explanation as to why I keep seeing these numbers – 123, 1234 and 222. Really, I feel I had no other choice but to delve further into these so-called angel numbers, so here goes.

Here are some of the responses I received to my internet inquiry for these numbers:

- According to Ryan Hart, who is a writer and researcher in the field of relationship science, which is the intersection between psychology and technology, he states that the number 1234 is a sign from your angels that they are with you and supporting you. This number is a reminder of the divine protection and support that is available to you at all times. He goes into much detail about this in his article titled: **1234 Angel Number**

Meaning and Spiritual Significance, Updated on June 24, 2022

- In numerology, the number 1234 is one of those numbers that is often referred to as a full-circle number. This is because the sum of its numbers, reduced to a single digit, is equal to 1, meaning it begins and ends in a 1 (1+2+3+4=10; 1+0=1). The powerful number 1 relates to concepts such as unity and beginnings while resonating with the energy of leadership. Angel number 1234 is commonly seen as a representation of simplicity.

- According to Psych News Daily, by Daria Burnett updated on DEC 13, 2022, the angel number 1234 is a powerful one indeed. If you keep seeing it, then something important is probably happening in your life. In brief, the 1234 angel number signifies that you are ready to let go of past beliefs and patterns that no longer serve you. And seeing this number repeatedly is a sign of good luck and positive energy coming your way, so your guardian angels are watching. In general, this is a sign that you can trust in the universe, and that you are on the right path.

- And according to the Ever Spiritual column titled: **Angel Number 1234 Meaning, Symbolism and Its Secret**, by Lisa Lindquist, updated: August 3, 2022, 1234 is a sequence number, so this could also mean you are on the right path to finding your life's purpose. This angel number's meaning may apply if you have been taking a new route in life or considering setting out on a new destination. Angel number 1234 is a reminder to take it one step at a time.   And breaking down the meaning of 1, 2, 3, and 4, when looking at the sequence of 1234, you can gather deeper meaning by understanding the meaning of each of its numbers. Each angel number has its special symbolism that, when put together it then pieces together the whole message. So, to fully understand the meaning of 1234, you must also understand the meaning of each number individually.

Researching this sequence of numbers had led me to many search results and for the most part they all tend to talk about a few key things:

- Positivity and keeping it simple
- Being on the right path
- Powerful message communicated from Angels and the Cosmos
- Biblically speaking it could also mean guidance from God and the Holy Spirit
- Seeing 123 / 1234 is also a message of encouragement

There is more research that point to the adding of each digit to arrive at your single angel number, such as 1+2+3+4=10, then 1+0 = 1 and therefore your angel number is 1. And still others have interpreted it as being the sum of each trait for angel numbers 1 – 4 and therefore you combine all of the traits of 1, 2, 3 and 4 and arrive at the meaning of seeing 1234.

As for repeatedly seeing the number 222, again according to Ryan Hart – the Biblical meaning of 222 is Love and Intelligence.

And in yet another result, I saw that it represented Love, Harmony and Divine protection.

Though I cannot deny that I have seen 1234, and 123 and even 222 for that matter, on many occasions, I will for the sake of this writing assume it to be all good news and to keep proceeding along my path, which as the meanings behind these numbers have described, as being on the right path.

But I am curious with how often I am seeing these numbers, and for that matter their various meanings; that it is basically having a root in being on the right path, encouragement, and divine protection. Even with this curiosity, I am content in my thinking that I am not in any real danger, that the path I have chosen is the correct one and that I am being encourage to continue forward in my search of discovery.

From a personal perspective, over the last 6+ years of my life, I have retired, I have seen the passing of my wife's parents and my mom, I have seen much growth in my children and grandchildren, I have become an author, and I have lost more of my hair with each passing year. Except for the passing of loved ones (and my hair loss), I truly love the current path that I am on.

I do not want to finish this chapter without mentioning the number Twelve (12). The number 12 by itself is a number that is represented within the Bible 187 times. The Bible has 12 tribes of Israel's, the 12 apostles of Jesus and in the Book of Kings in the Hebrew bible, Elisha built the alter of 12 stones for the offering.

Additionally, in science there are many references to the number 12 and it is the number given to represent space and time. That's why these two numbers (1&2) when added equal 3 which represents the third-dimension plane in which we exist, as well as the number 3 has many biblical references such as the Holy Trinity (Father, Son and the Holy Ghost).

And the number 12 is used in Physics for the numeric formula for the masses of particles called the "Alpha-12" mass formula. Time is even measured by two groups of 12 hours, and there is 12 inches in a foot, just as there are 12 items in a dozen and 12 dozen in a gross. And there are 12 pairs of ribs in the human body.

The Zodiac has 12 signs, and there are 12 months in a year. The Sumerians counted by 12 using the hand, knuckles and pads on 4 fingers. Example shows how it was done.

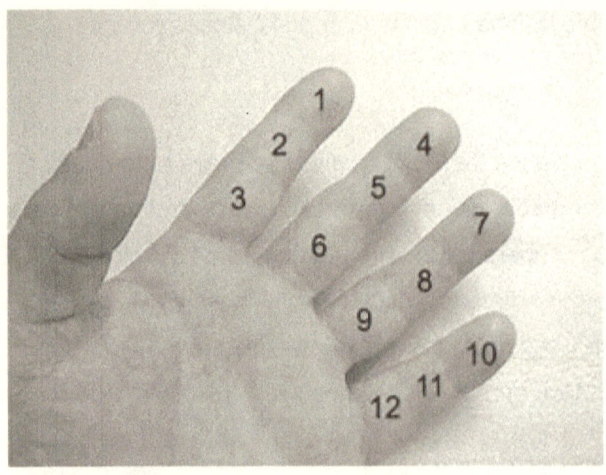

The Knights Templar, today associated with Freemasonry and the Masonic Order, also engaged in the number 12. Their High Priest, while in ceremony, would wear a Masonic Chest Plate with 12 Stones, said to represent the 12 tribes of Israel.

Even the UFO-ologists cannot get away from the number 12 as when Truman first selected a group to study the phenomenon, he called that group The Majestic 12, and their purpose was to study extraterrestrial beings and UFO's occurrences.

The troposphere is the atmosphere's lowest layer, and it extends upwards to 12 miles above the surface of our planet. It is the layer where most of the Earth's weather occurs. Then there are the 12 grades of traditional US schooling (grades 1 – 12). And let's not forget the 12 Days of Christmas, and 12 jurors in a typical court.

The human body has 114 chakras points that represent divine energy and the network of energy flow. However, 12 of them are addressed as the major chakras. And mythologically speaking the 12 gods on Mount Olympus, and the 12 labors of Hercules.

Attempting to finish this chapter, to draw a conclusion from all of this information regarding the repeated seeing of these numbers, as I have called Signs, has led me to yet another question – **is there any significant to these so-called angel numbers and my repeatedly seeing them, or is this just all coincidence?** Perhaps it is nothing more than mere exuberance given to old stories passed down through history, a musing of the times kept alive through repeated telling of such phenomenon.

I cannot say at this time that I have an answer to this question. I cannot, however, deny that I am seeing and continue to see 123 and 1234 repeatedly to this day, even though it's meaning is not really one I would have typically contemplated at the time.

Whatever the case, what are referred to as angel numbers are further observed even today with much awareness and weight given to the meaning behind the observation. Going forward, especially after my research here, I will be giving more thought as to the reasoning of why I may be seeing certain numbers.

Could there be something more, perhaps a message contained in the viewing of the number(s) at that time, perhaps a Sign that contains an important message that I need to pay specific attention to, or is it nothing more than mere coincidence. The forever analyst in me will not, at least for now, ignore these continued observations, the potential for a message and the resultant consequence of same.

By the way I had Chinese food for dinner the other night and my fortune cookie read – 'Never ignore a gut feeling, but never believe that it's enough'. Things that make you go – Hmmmm!

One last thing, as I was finishing up this chapter and thinking I had it completed, I came upon a news article in one of my online news feeds. The news feed came from Fox News and was originally published on December 27, 2022 by Nicole Pelletiere. The article was titled: **What are 'Angel Numbers' and why do people keep seeing them?**

Though this article was originally published on December 27, it for some reason showed up in one of my newsfeeds on the exact day (January 4th) that I finished this chapter of the book. Coincidence or yet another Sign perhaps? Again – things that make you go Hmmmm!

Having thought I was totally finished with this chapter; I am yet again being pulled back into it. Sunday the 8th of January 2023, the Buffalo Bills played their first football game since their safety #3 Damar Hamlin had a cardiac arrest on the field on (01/02/2023) while playing the Cincinnati Bengals. Since that time, he has been in intensive care in the Cleveland Clinic Hospital. The Bills team, the media, and for that matter most of the nation had offered up prayers and well wishes for Damar Hamlin.

The Sunday game saw the Buffalo Bills playing the New England Patriots. The Bills and for that matter all 32 NFL teams were sporting the #3 in support of Damar Hamlin. On the opening kickoff to the Bills, Nyheim Hines returned the opening kickoff for a score – a 96-yard run! Well, if you were looking at this from a pure numerology perspective some might say that taking the 96 yard return and separating the numbers of 9 and 6, the subtracting the 6 from the 9 equals 3 and that is Damar Hamlin's jersey number. Let's look at this game a bit deeper and as they say 'let's look at the numbers'.

The Bills' specials team unit collaborated to block for and score that kick-return touchdown for the first time in three (3) years and three (3) months. Currently playing Hamlin's position of Safety is a third (3rd) string person, and the Bills scored three (3) interceptions in the game.

However, the Bills performance was far from being what you would call pristine, as the Bills managed to lose two fumbles and threw for an interception to tally, you guessed it, three (3) turnovers. So, I really do have to ask why so many 3's showing up in these stats? As we all know the game was dedicated to Damar Hamlin #3.

The Bills, its coaching staff, and for that matter, the Bengals all prayed on the field that day following Damar's hit and his resultant collapse. We also know that there have been many prayers since for the well-being and recovery of Damar.

Was this game scripted as some nay-sayers offered up on various social media platforms, or was this in some way Angelic or even Divine Intervention? I leave that up to you all to decide and as for me I already know what I believe about all of this. And as they say the third times a charm!

By the way on January 9, 2023 Damar Hamlin was released from the Cleveland Clinic and transferred to a Buffalo NY hospital. And on January 11, 2023 Damar was released from the Buffalo hospital for continued recuperation and rehab at home.

Since his time in the hospital, Damar has been an outspoken spokesperson for heart health and CPR training. Hamlin has launched the "3 for Heart CPR Challenge" campaign in partnership with the American Heart Association. This campaign is designed to increase CPR awareness, education and training.

We are now heading into the 2023/2024 professional football season and Damar Hamlin, as of May 23, 2023 has returned to practice at the Buffalo Bills Offseason Program – commonly referred to as the OTA's.

One final note here. A few weeks ago, early June of 2023, while I was driving home, a car abruptly pulled in front of me in traffic. He was so close in making it into my lane that I needed to quickly and firmly apply my brakes. My initial thought was one that is not appropriate in mixed company, and frankly I was angry with his careless driving. That was until I saw his license plate. The license read KEV followed by a series of numbers.

Most people call me by my first name – Kevin. However, some really good close friends do call me Kev. Immediately seeing the license plate caused me to take pause once again. Was someone close to me sending me a message – a Sign as it were? Thinking that this might be the case, and not just another coincidence, I jotted down the plate number and continued to drive home. I will not divulge that plate numbers digits in order to preserve anonymity of the car owner.

Once back home, and after relating the story to my wife, I sat down at the computer to begin my search on the number. I found several references to the number, with some stating to reference the meaning of each of the individual numbers, other saying to add up to a single digit, and still other results showing meaning for the specific number itself.

The referenced license plate number as viewed in its entirety had many references from numerology, biblical, astrological, spiritual and more. I have compiled a list of its meaning from several of these sources. They are:

- Turn your ideas and thoughts into your new reality
- Trust in your talents and abilities
- Thoughts and feelings create reality
- You're on the right path and Angels are guiding
- Hard work and determination bring you financial stability
- Trust in the power of prayer and faith
- And overall, a message of encouragement, abundance and empowerment.

These were interesting results from the search. Some of the results even read like the message from a fortune cookie. Was this perhaps a Sign for me, a message to stay the course of action, and giving me encouragement? For now, I will continue to ponder this, but I do have to admit, that car cutting me off and having that license plate, definitely caught my attention. Coincidence – perhaps, but as we've discussed – the Veil is thinner than we imagine.

5.3 ANGEL NUMBERS – A FURTHER UNDERSTANDING

Special Note: There are many references to Angel Numbers upon any search of the Internet. I suggest that you do your own research if you wish to gain a fuller understanding regarding the multitude of information encompassing Angel Numbers.

The following information is extracted from: *Angel Numbers - The Complete Online Guide for Angel Numbers (guardian-angel-reading.com)* (https://www.guardian-angel-reading.com/blog-of-the-angels/angel-numbers/#C4)

Angel numbers and numerology are often used interchangeably, but there are subtle differences between the two. Numerology is the study of the energy and meaning behind numbers, while angel numbers refer more to the messages contained within the numbers that are thought to be delivered by angels. Angel numbers are seen as a set or repetitive digits and are usually thought to be a sign from the divine. Numerology attempts to understand the connection between the physical and spiritual realms through the meaning of the number.

Numerology is backed by the doctrine that the universe is mathematically precise and that every number has a precise and clear meaning different from another. Numerology also states that each number 1-9, are called the "master numbers" and each one has a very distinct and significant meaning on its own.

The key is to remember that when you see a number repeatedly, you are being communicated with. It will not matter whether you understand the meaning because it is said that your subconscious mind will understand everything for you.

Meaning of single digit numbers:
Each of the numbers between 0 and 9 is considered a core number. They hold specific meanings that relate to deep and important aspects of our lives.

The following is taken from the link at the beginning of this section. However, there's much to learn about Angel Numbers and Numerology if you intend to put these learnings into practice.

Core Number 0
When you see 0 in an angel number, you know that the message is related to your spirituality. But this number also amplifies the meaning of its surrounding numbers. For example, in the number 50, the meaning of the number 5 would be made stronger by the presence of the 0.

Core Number 1
This number primarily focuses on new beginnings and positivity. You should therefore look to those opportunities with optimism.

Core Number 2
Remain adaptable, flexible, and considerate, and your prayers will be answered. If you're working towards goals, with help

of number 2, you'll find that they also connect to your life goal and soul mission. Be patient!

Core Number 3

When you see number 3, it's a sign that your angels are trying to get your attention. You've may have taken a step in the wrong direction and they wish to help you. Trust your intuition.

Core Number 4

When it comes to 4 as a core number we see that it holds two meanings. First, it is a reminder that your angels are always here and always ready to offer support and guidance. Secondly, you should put proper planning into everything that you do. Laying the foundations is one of the most important steps.

Core Number 5

The number 5 suggests that changes are coming your way and may already be in motion. Your angels are reminding you to look to these changes with a positive and optimistic attitude.

Core Number 6

Six represents balance and harmony and remind you to find a balance between your material and spiritual pursuits. Don't allow material desires to negatively impact your spiritual development.

Core Number 7

When you see the number 7 it means that your angels are happy with the decisions you've been making. They are encouraging you to continue along your path.

You should also embrace your spiritual gifts by trying to help others along their path as well.

Core Number 8
Embrace positive affirmations, thoughts, and abundance with number 8. These will be key aspects of your journey as they will allow you to bring more positivity into the world.

You'll find that karma will be paying off soon. So, if you've put in the necessary work, you will notice the rewards for your efforts.

Core Number 9
The number 9 represents the end of a chapter or cycle. This could mean the end of a job or hobby, or it could be something larger like the end of a long spiritual journey as you enter the next phase of your life path.

What is my angel number?
Does each person have their own Angel number – well it has been written that each person does indeed have an Angel Number and that it is calculated by using their birth date.

First, take all the numbers from your date of birth and add them together. For example, let's used the date of a person born on

May 4th, 1993 (05/04/1993). Begin by adding all the individual numbers: 0 + 5 + 0 + 4 + 1 + 9 + 9 + 3 = 31.

Next, we would further reduce this number by adding the digits together: 3 + 1 = 4. So, the angel number for the person with this birthdate would be 4.

When you see repetitions of number sequences relating to your birth date, you should know that the Angels want you to focus on who you are and what is your sole purpose in life. They perhaps are leading you to further examine what the purpose of your existence is, and what you can and are willing to achieve in life?

Through this message, the Angels are trying to further direct you in the realization that you have a separate and unique identity and that you should not be comparing yourself to others.

Much study needs to be devoted to the area of numerology and Angel Numbers, but suffice it to say that when you repeatedly see number sequences throughout your daily life, then know that you are being communicated with by those who have been described as Angels or spirits.

"The top experts in the world are ardent students. The Day you stop learning, you're definitely not an expert."
Brendon Buchard

6 RESEARCH FROM MANY NOTABLE EXPERTS

Christopher Kerr, MD, PhD

Dr. Kerr began his hospice doctoring as a part-time weekend staff doctor and is now the Chief Medical Officer and Chief Executive Officer for Hospice & Palliative Care Buffalo.

Dr. Kerr's background in research has evolved from bench science toward the human experience of illness as witnessed from the bedside. Today he can be found interacting with his patients with utmost compassion during their remaining life, while his analyst's mind continues to research and document the dying patients' dreams and visions. Although medically ignored, these near-universal experiences often provide comfort and meaning, as well as insight into the life led and the death anticipated.

Dr. Kerr and the research team have spent years researching the impact of ELE's on hospice patients and their families. By understanding the nature of these experiences and the role they play in the dying process, Dr. Kerr and his team are working to improve the quality of hospice care in Buffalo and beyond.

Visitation dreams have been studied for decades and as I started this chapter with words about Dr. Kerr and his work at the Buffalo Hospice, he and his team have interviewed and documented the final weeks of life of 1,500+ hospice patients

181

over the last 10+ years. What they have discovered was that 80 percent of those interviewed reported having very vivid dreams and/or visions prior to the time of their deaths.

"It's life affirming, I can tell you that," Dr. Kerr said, noting that the dreams seem to make passing away less scary for his patients. For the dying patient these dreams are detailed and real and very often bring comfort and peace. This dying process teaches us that the best parts of living are never lost.

As Dr. Kerr described in his TED talk: *I See Dead People: Dreams and Visions of the Dying* – "dying is a paradox between the body dying and the spiritual soul being alive and vibrant". Perhaps it is the viewing of the thin veil between our living world and the spiritual world – or what has often been referred to as the afterlife.

Dr. Kerr has been a guest on podcasts discussing his experience as a doctor of a Hospice care facility in Buffalo NY. He also wrote a book titled: *Death is But a Dream – Finding Hope and Meaning at Life's End*.

After watching his TED talk and listening to some of his podcasts, I decided to purchase Dr. Kerr's book. Reading it I began to understand that dying is a process, and like most processes the process of dying has a starting and an ending point. The overall process can be quick or take some time dependent upon many circumstances, but there are indeed sign posts along the way of the process steps that indicate when one is approaching the proverbial death's door.

After my digestion of Dr. Kerr's talks and his book, I found that I had several questions that I wanted to discuss with the doctor. I knew I needed to find a way to talk with him so I began by searching out his contact information. Knowing that he was working at the Hospice and Palliative Care center of Buffalo made for an easy internet search. Upon finding his information I immediately sent an email of introduction to him. After a few back-and-forth emails, Dr. Kerr was willing to have an online video chat regarding several questions I had.

On March 7, 2023 I met online with Dr. Kerr and after exchanging pleasantries we got right down to business.

Dr. Kerr, Chris as he asked me to call him, was very forthcoming with answers to my questions including one where I asked if the medical community had embraced his studies and the papers he has written regarding his work with the hospice patients. To be honest, from what I have researched I expected to hear that they are indeed warming to the concept of ELE's that the good doctor and his staff have documented over the last 10 – 15 years. However, Chris was not in agreement with that thought and stated "there is still much work to be done."

From my short time speaking with Chris, I was further convinced of a few things. One was that I found in Chris a very approachable person, willing to openly discuss and share the data he and his team have gathered over the years from observing their patients. Second, the good doctor was very concerned for his patient's comfort and safety. He was not doing this research for notoriety or fame, but he was conducting the research to learn more about the dying process, with the desired outcome perhaps being an ability to approach with dignity the process of dying that his patients were experiencing.

I believe it is important to also note that none of this would have been made possible without the consent of the patient and their families. From reading Chris's book, seeing his TED talks, and viewing the DVD, his patients appear very open to telling their stories, and to the video taping of same. The patients' stories, told in their own words, emphasize the importance of understanding the dying process, and preserving the dignity of them throughout this process.

There were some questions I had that dealt with the bereaved family and friends. I wanted to understand if Chris and his team did any studies of the bereaved after the death of their loved ones. Chris had given me a paper he co-authored called: **The Impact of Dreams on Bereavement: A Survey of Hospice Caregivers.** This paper described the results of a survey given to 278 bereaved persons regarding their own perspective of the relation between dreams and the mourning process. From the survey results – 60% of the participants felt that their dreams impacted the bereavement process.

The total results of the survey indicated that 55.3% found the dreams pleasant, 31.1% found them both pleasant and somewhat disturbing, 6.8% found them disturbing and 6.8% were other.   These results are not dissimilar to those I have read in various other online articles. For the most part, these findings are almost a decade old and from my most recent online searching there does not appear to be a more recent detailed study of this nature conducted, at least none that I could find.

Abstract of the Dr. Kerr co-authored paper can be found here: https://journals.sagepub.com/doi/10.1177/1049909113479201

See also Appendix A2 for interview questions and responses.

Carl Jung, MD
Carl Jung, a Swiss psychologist (1875-1961), studied visitation dreams and their deeper meanings which has led to what is now known as Jungian analytical psychology. It is an approach that takes a person's body, mind, and soul into consideration when trying to uncover the meaning behind their dreams.

Jung's approach was meant to help people make their unconscious thoughts and experiences into conscious ones by helping them analyze their lives, their dreams and fantasies.

Sigmond Freud, MD
Sigmond Freud (1856-1939) and his theories about dreams were much more encompassing and is probably the most well-known and perhaps infamous – theory of dreams.

At the turn of the 20th century, Sigmund Freud published his book, **The Interpretation of Dreams**, arguing that our dreams are nothing more than our own wishes that we are looking to fulfil in our waking lives. Some of these wishes are relatively innocent, and in these cases our dreams picture the wish just as it is.

However, he argues, there are other wishes that are so unacceptable to us that our dreams censor them. Such wishes are maybe suppressed by the conscious mind only then to turn up in our dreams in a manner that may be foreign or in some way bizarre. But with the help of a psychoanalyst and methods like free association, Freud argued that the wish behind the dream could be discovered.

I have included this section on Freud as many people have heard of Freud and his research on dreams. However, despite the theory's fame and influence on other psychological theories it has been largely discredited in recent years, and thoroughly debunked by modern dream scientists.

Patrick McNamara Ph.D.

Patrick McNamara is the Associate Professor of Neurology at Boston University School of Medicine and the author of numerous books and articles on the science of dreams. He received his B.A. in Psychology, from Boston University, was awarded a Ph.D. in Behavioral Neuroscience (Human Neuropsychology), also from Boston University, and did a

Postdoctoral Fellowship at the Aphasia Research Center, Boston VA Medical Center.

Dr. McNamara has over fifteen (15) years of experience working on the problem of the nature and function of dreaming. Dr McNamara has steadily increased his work on dreams and has now published over 30 scientific papers on dreams as well as several books.

He has pondered about: how many people and what kind of people report visitation dreams; do the bereaved have visitation shortly after the death or can it happen years afterward; and what effects do visitation dreams have on that of the dreamer?

As Dr McNamara has stated, and paraphrased here: the dream structure is not disorganized or bizarre. Instead, visitation dreams are typically clear, vivid, intense, and are experienced as real visits when the dreamer awakens. The dreamer is often changed by the experience, and there may be a resolution of the grieving process and/or a wider spiritual perspective.

Given these basic characteristics of visitation dreams, such dreams must be considered among the most remarkable and most important categories of dreams. As mentioned above they continue to be understudied.

This information is paraphrased and condensed from an article on Dr. McNamara in Psychology Today October 8, 2011, titled:

Visitation Dreams – Can dreams carry messages from loved-ones who have died?

From this author's viewpoint based upon what I have both experienced and read, there are commonalities or themes from these Visitation Dreams. For example, a major common theme is that these dreams are very vivid in detail, real and lifelike. The dreams are described as mostly peaceful and usually bring a sense of comfort to the dreamer.

Other characteristics include the clarity of the dream allowing the detail to be easily remembered. The dreamer can usually recall the dream details hours, days and even weeks after. And one more characteristic was that the overwhelming percentage of the dreams left the bereaved feeling that their departed loved one was now out of pain, at peace, and calm.

Overall, the appearance of a deceased person in our dreams can be a sign of love; that they are with us and perhaps watching over us. You may also feel reassured and comforted after they have paid a visit, even if it is only for a brief moment.

And to bring this full circle – in today's parlance these visitation dreams, and for that matter, ELE dreams, have also been referred to as 'Thin Places'. According to **Rev. Dr. Mark D. Roberts** in **THIN PLACES: A BIBLICAL INVESTIGATION,** "A thin place is a place where the boundary between heaven and earth is especially thin. It is a place where we can sense the divine more readily."

Many end of life experiences have included the feeling that the dying person was stepping in two worlds at the same time. Others have also described it as two energy forces coming together.

For me the journey getting to this point has been one of wonder, imagination, insight, and exploration. I know that I am not yet done exploring the possibilities and the mysteries of the dying process. Whatever your viewpoints are, one thing is for sure, there is much more yet to learn.

Through all of the interviews, hearing several people's stories and having my own experiences, one thing I know for sure is that *the Veil is thinner than we imagine.*

"The most beautiful experience we can have is the mysterious. It is the fundamental emotion that stands at the cradle of true art and true science."
Albert Einstein

7 SUMMATION AND CONCLUSION

How do you sum up and conclude a book like this? These Signs I have spoken about are not just one-shot affairs, the Angel numbers do not just appear once, the Visitation Dreams do not just happen one night and the ongoing assistance/help when called upon maybe never ending (personally for me it's still happening).

Just today, I was on the treadmill, and happened to look down at the readout on the column and there in all its glory the number 12:34. My treadmill rotates through the readouts that track the time walked, the calories burned, how many burned in an hour, the incline, the pace I am walking, the miles walked so far, and my pulse. Why out of all those rotated numbers did I then see 12:34 show up?

Can this all just be coincidence? Can it be my imagination run amuck? As they say in the Queen's song Bohemian Rhapsody – *Is this the real life? Is this just fantasy? ...Open your eyes, look up to the sky and see!*

I have pondered many times if this was all just my imagination, did I really miss seeing the Airliner Motel picture all those times while I looked around the dining room table. Did the novelty toy of my brother's actually go off that one day? And what about my dreams, the hummingbird and butterfly visit, my wife's earrings and on and on and on. Did this 'imagination' also extend to my wife and friends who witnessed the earrings, or extend to my daughter and her children finding the candy wrappers?

Am I now somehow the crazy one, or am I the lucky one, to be counted amongst those that can say they have been visited by past loved ones? Am I the fortunate one that can state unequivocally that I have been helped by past loved ones in solving a situation I was having?

What about those experiences of my dear friends who have chosen to share their stories with me. What about Dr. Kerr and his 1500+ reviews of hospice patients having visitation dreams? How about Doug, Kari, Ashley and the King Air plane with the pilot dying? What about Brian and Ron's events at the Twin Towers on 9/11? What about Ed Currie's angelic vision in the condo doorway and the impact it had on his life? How about coach Johnson and J-Mac and their stories? Are they all just crazy too?

Having experienced so many of these events in my lifetime, especially the later years, I cannot deny to myself that indeed these happenings are real. They have made me evermore alert to my surroundings, cognizant of and vigilant for their continued occurrence.

Dr. Kerr, and others have documented countless times, the dear departed and their dreams. The vivid and blissful images of past loved ones bringing comfort to those in their dying days. Can these be written off as mere coincidence, an over active imagination as they near death?

I have saved the following until now as I did not think these next experiences as being Signs, but upon reflection maybe they were. Signs perhaps that I was being watched over for some clandestine reason.

Being an active child of perhaps 8 or 9, I was visiting with my cousins at their house, which was across a stream just off of the road. To get to the house we needed to cross a one-way, wooden plank bridge, that for the most part really needed some shoring up, or with the creek water running low, you could drive through the stream bed and up the bank.

While visiting there, my cousins and I went down to the stream to play, and while I walked across the bridge, not really looking where I was going, I got too close to the side and fell off. Needless to say, I tumbled down to the ground receiving several scrapes and a pretty nasty gash to my left leg.

Bleeding, and in pain, I managed to pull myself up along the creek bank, and was assisted there by my cousins. The lucky part was that had I gone another couple feet along the bridge before falling, I would have tumbled down another 8 – 10 feet into the water and could have suffered something more severe, perhaps even life threatening.

This was not going to be my last brush with near disaster. For, at my age of 14, my dad's job was transferred to Minnesota. Our first winter there was so brutally cold that after school one day I wanted to get the house warm before my parents came home from work so I started a fire in the two fireplaces in the house. The wood being wet was giving me some problems with it lighting so I thought – I'll use some lighter fluid. Finding that it was empty, and without giving it much thought I grabbed the gasoline can and doused the wood.

I then was able to light the wood and it was burning for a while. Because of how wet the wood was, it soon was dying out, so back to the gasoline. I doused the wood again only this time the flame traveled back to the gas can, and I stood there seeing the nozzle of the can with a flame coming from it. Quickly I cupped the nozzle with my hand and put the flame out. Feeling lucky, but still scared, I set the gas can outside of the house.

What stopped that gas can from blowing up? Well, I am sure there is some physics that's alluding me as to why it did not blow up, but I for one felt extremely lucky.

Again, these were not the only times that perhaps I could have been staring at the grim reaper. I had three close experiences with BBQ Grills – with one time having the flame traveling down the fill line and heading right towards the propane tank. The other two were when the grill did not light and I leaned into the grill to hear if the gas was flowing, when the person with me decided to also hit the ignitor trying once again to light the grill.

Well on both of those last two occurrences, the grill lit and the flame rushed up around me. Both of those occasions not only severely singed my beard and mustache, but also managed to remove my eyebrows. For some reason on both of those times I had my eyes closed, and perhaps lucky for me that I did.

There have been other situations too, a bit less dramatic than what I have already mentioned here, but none the less all of these actions could have been much worse. Luck cannot be the only term I can use to describe them. Was there something more to all of this – have I been watched over by past loved ones, by a 'Clarence' as was the case of George Bailey in *It's a Wonderful Life* **(**'teacher says – every time a bell rings an Angel gets its wings'**).** I cannot say with any degree of certainty, I can only add this to all of the other interesting events in my life.

To sum it up, I feel like there are only a few possible explanations for all of this. One is that these experiences that I have described in this book are real, or two – it was all a coincidence made possible by the persons activity combined with their and other's imagination.

If I were to agree with the second thought then perhaps, I am living in a state of mind where I need to be seen by competent people for evaluation. Otherwise, if I believe in the first thought occurring, then I also have to believe in an afterlife; that in some way the departed can indeed communicate with us.

Believing in the afterlife, and following the logic here, I must then believe in the premise that we are therefore watched over while we fulfil our life's purpose. Furthermore, thinking about my life's purpose and for that matter the whole premise of '**why am I here**', as well as all that I have experienced to date with these many life events, I must admit that I have not yet come to any conclusions that can tie all of this together in a somewhat neat bow beyond what may be called spiritual and religious in nature.

But I do believe this with all certainty, we are not alone. We are the living amongst the departed. We do have a purpose. We are directed – if we allow it, while also being watched over. Our road may not always be an easy one as we may not be those that are rich, or famous, or good looking, or in any other way counted among the popular. But we are equally just as important where things really matter.

Therefore, my conclusion is that whatever you might want to call the events that have happened to me and my friends; whatever you might think about those I have interviewed and the experts I wrote about within this book; whatever else you might want to assign to these happenings; my alertness to them and faith in them – has only been strengthened.

"There are many truths of which the full meaning cannot be realized until personal experience has brought it home."
John S. Mill

I cannot and will not tell you what to think about them, I can only ask that you view them with an open mind. To be ever diligent for the discovery of your own Signs, and to what these Signs may have to tell or in other ways direct you.

Question them, analyze them, even doubt them at times if you will, but continue to receive them in the manner that they were meant for you. Do not deny them just because it may not seem logical, nor be fearful of them because you do not know what or why you are receiving them.

"Fear can keep us up all night, but faith makes one fine pillow" – Phillip Gulley

Think about the world around you, the time of your receiving of the Sign and what it could possibly be meaning in its delivery. Stay alert to the various Signs and above all else remain in faith that there is much more to this world than meets the eye. For as Socrates has said *"the unexamined life is not worth living"*.

S I G N S

The Veil is Thinner than we Imagine!

"Never become so much of an expert that you stop learning. View life as a continuous learning experience."
Denis Waitley

Appendix A1: THREE DAYS AFTER DEATH

"The Spirit lingers for three (3) days and walks the Earth", was a message that my mother had delivered to me on more than one occasion. I often wondered where she had formed that belief, and because she never told me I decided to do some research to see where that belief could have started. Below are some of the notes about religious teachings and interpretations that were discovered as a result of that research.

Jewish interpretation:
There is some conflicting belief about the Jewish soul, or spirit, lingering for three days after death. While some believe it is up to seven days, others believe that the soul can be restless for 12 months. These beliefs are attributed to the ancient wisdom contained in the Kabbalah.

According to the Talmud: When people die, the soul will go to heaven (Genesis Rabbah 14:9), but first it stays near the body for three days, hoping that it will return to life. After three days, the soul will then return to God to await the time of resurrection (Babylonian Talmud Sanhedrin 90b-91a).

Christianity discussion on Jesus's resurrection after 3 days:
From Biblical (KJV) writings regarding Jesus's death: There are several reasons it is significant Jesus was dead for three days

before His resurrection. First, resurrection after three days of death proved to Jesus' opponents that He truly rose from the dead. Why? According to Jewish tradition, a person's soul/spirit remained with his/her dead body for three days. After three days, the soul/spirit departed. If Jesus' resurrection had occurred on the same day or even the next day, it would have been easier for his enemies to argue he had never truly died. Significantly, Jesus waited several days after Lazarus had died before he came to resurrect him so no one could deny the miracle (John 11:38–44).

Matthew 12:40 (NIV) states that – "For as Jonah was three days and three nights in the belly of a huge fish, so the son of man will be three days and three nights in the heart of the Earth."

Discussion by Swami Sivananda and his Hindu belief:
'The soul which passes out of the body after death is termed 'Preta', one that is bound on its march to the Beyond. The soul in its disembodied form hovers about its original and familiar places for ten days. It is in the form of a ghost during these ten days.

The astral body takes shape from day to day with the formation of the head, eyes, and other limbs of the Linga Sarira, fed and nourished by the sesamum and water poured out in libation over the stones which represent the ancestors.'
https://hinduism.stackexchange.com/questions

Further research found in the Hindu text, the "Bhagavad Gita" – The Song of God – says of the soul,
It is not born; it does not die;

Having been, it will never not be.
Unborn, eternal, constant and primordial;
It is not killed, when the body is killed.

This information was taken from the article: *In the midst of deep grief, a scholar writes how Hindu rituals taught her to let go*, written October 1, 2020. That article can be found at: https://theconversation.com/in-the-midst-of-deep-grief-a-scholar-writes-how-hindu-rituals-taught-her-to-let-go-145370

Japanese culture and the belief about Death
According to traditional Japanese beliefs, all humans have a spirit or soul called a reikon. When a person dies, the reikon leaves the body and enters a form of purgatory, where it waits for the proper funeral and post-funeral rites to be performed so that it may join its ancestors. This can be a few days to complete. If this is done correctly, the reikon is believed to be a protector of the living family and to return yearly in August during the Obon Festival to receive thanks.

Further understandings from my research:
Through my research I discovered much more, however, nothing conclusive to answer the question of why my mom thought that the spirit walks the Earth for 3 days after death of the body. I can only surmise that because mom was Christian, perhaps she interpreted the fact that Jesus rose 3 days after his death, to be that the spirit remains on Earth for 3 days. Whatever her reasoning for this belief was, I may never know until the day I too cross over to the other side of the Veil.

Appendix A2: Dr. Kerr Interview Questions

The following are the questions that I used during my interview with Dr. Kerr, along with his responses. The questions, and a brief explanation were forwarded to Dr. Kerr prior to my call with him. Here is the complete document I sent and his responses, that I recorded from our conversation.

My intention was to also have the hospice center nurses answer these questions. Because of the business dynamics of the organization, we would have to seek permission to authorize that to happen, and it could take some time to acquire the permission. Therefore, I elected not to pursue it at this time.

Document sent starts here:
For background, I am writing a book that starts after the passing of an individual and how they (the departed) are felt, seen, and experienced by the bereaved. This book is about what I have come to title (a working title at this point) **Signs**, and chronicles the various experiences my wife and I have had with the afterlife - relatives that have come for a 'dream visit' or in other ways have let us know they are ok.

You have described your patients ELE visions and dreams as being vivid in detail, realistic, often presenting a calming and accepting feeling amongst the dying. Those same descriptions are also told by the bereaved of their experiences. The bereaved often have their own experiences too. Some of these experiences start right away upon their loved one's death, and some of them last for weeks/months thereafter.

Though this may not be in your direct realm of research, I feel that I can acquire from you, knowledge that could assist me both in my understanding of our visitations as well as help with my writing about the subject that may then help many others through the reading of my book.

The following are just a few questions that might help to guide/direct our conversation.

1.) Within your book and TED talks, you speak about the dying process and End of Life Experiences of your patients, and you have chronicled over 1500 of their stories. Have you had any follow up conversations with their families as to what they have experienced both before and after their loved ones have passed away?
Response: *Dr. Kerr: They did not and have not spent time with the bereaved. I recommend you review what psychotherapist William Peters has to say about the subject.* (my note: Peters has written papers and a book re: this topic.)

2.) Have you or your staff experienced any dreams, or visions or have you had any other experiences with those who have died – after their death?

Response: *Dr. Kerr is unaware of this; however, he admits that the question has not yet been asked.*

3.) Have you or your staff chronicled any 'Out of Body Experiences – OBE's' with those that were dying? Was any of that researched as part of your patients ELE's?
Response: *Dr. Kerr is unaware of this; however, he admits that the question has not yet been asked.*

4.) Have you researched what other cultures both now and historically have thought about dreams and the dying process? For example, the Japanese call it 'Pick up' dreams and the word Dream in Japanese means 'hope or aspiration'. The Aboriginies believed that their ancestors dreamed everything into existence and they believe that dreams connect them with their departed ancestors.
Response: *Dr. Kerr has not researched (sic) to any large extent other cultural beliefs and practices, but he does believe that this permeates throughout many cultures and throughout history.*

5.) Within your book, the dying youth talked about pets – mostly dogs. Have any of your patients ever talked (*sic*) about seeing birds or other animals before their deaths? Have the families of the departed spoken about having any of their own experiences with animals, etc. after their loved one's deaths?
Response: Dr. Kerr: *From our studies, about 35% of the dying patients have seen pets and animals at end of their life.*

6.) How has the medical/science community embraced your research?

Response: *Dr Kerr: From what I have seen they really have not yet embraced this.*

7.) What would you advise me to think about or not think about – to include or not include – in my writing of this book?

Response: *Dr. Kerr: Perhaps tighten your focus.* (My note: I gave Dr. Kerr several of the ideas I was researching for the book prior to his response. He felt there were too many.)

8.) Will you be OK with me quoting you within my book, taking quotes from your book or from your TED talks? I will share those sections of the book with you prior to publishing, to make sure I have quoted you correctly.

Response: *Dr. Kerr: Yes, I have no problem with you quoting me, my book, my DVD or my TED talks.*

Other research included:

Dr. Kerr sent me his DVD titled: **Death is but a dream**, and I purchased his book titled: **Death is but a dream – Finding Hope and Meaning at Life's End.** Additionally, I researched and read his co-authored paper titled: **The Impact of Dreams of the Deceased on Bereavement: A Survey of Hospice Caregivers. Lastly, I have viewed his TED talk titled: I See Dead People: Dreams and Visions of the Dying.**

APPENDIX A3: CULTURAL BELIEFS

Historically-speaking, our departed coming to us in dreams are some of the earliest transcribed accounts of dream life. Aristotle (384 BC), a Greek philosopher and scientist, one of the greatest intellectual figures of Western history, mentioned them.

Lucretius (1st century BC), a Latin poet and philosopher, also mentions them in part to comment on the widespread folk psychology that the characters in people's dreams actually seem to be the spirits of the departed.

Given the pronouncement of Greek philosophers it's no wonder that in the ancient world Mythology – Thanatos (God of the Dead) and Hypnos (God of Dreams) are brothers.

The Vikings or Norseman (Norse), late 700's – late 1000's (AD), took dreams quite seriously. While they acknowledged that some dreams were random and meaningless (and called them draumskrok, "dream-nonsense"), other dreams were held to possess enormous significance.

Dreams could sometimes foretell the future. Their ability to do so went hand in hand with the Norse view that all events were directed by fate; and since they believed that the future was preordained, it could be known in advance. They had a firm belief that dreams could provide a means of contact between living humans and otherworldly beings such as the dead, elves, land spirits, and deities. Such beings often bore an important message for the dreamers, and sometimes even struck a deal with them that led to tangible benefits in waking life.

I could go on to cite ancient China and Egypt, as well as hundreds of contemporary indigenous cultures, who also have made the link between dreams and ancestors, but suffice to say that dreams have always been noted as a natural place for the deceased to mingle with us.

An article by Ryan Hurd, author of several books on dreaming and blogger of same, discusses **How Dreams of Bereavement Reach Out to Us** (title of article). Perhaps a misnomer is that the visitation dream is really a bereavement dream. Ryan describes the difference between Visitation and Bereavement dreams as (paraphrase here):

> *Like visitation dreams, bereavement dreams center around an encounter with the deceased, consisting of a meeting, an exchange, and an ending of the dream. Unlike visitation dreams, however, bereavement dreams tend to come quickly after the death of a loved one. Sometimes the night afterward, sometimes a week or month, or even three months later. Bereavement dreams indicate that grieving is still a major factor and influence upon the living.*

"Some bereavement dreams do not have the cognitive clarity or lucidity that other visitation dreams have; instead, they can be highly emotional, resulting in waking up in grief and tears, sometimes mixed with elation". These dreams are not always positive and they can be disturbing and confrontational.

The following comes from an article titled: *Here's What These Ancient Cultures Believed About Dreams 2/22/2019,* By Deb Powers as posted on the *'Dream Tending site by Stephen Aizenstat, PHD'.*

In ancient **Egyptian** times, the dream world existed between the land of the living and the world on the other side, a world inhabited by deities and the spirits of the dead. Dreams were communications from those entities.

Because they felt that dreams were so significant, many Egyptians were meticulous about recording their dreams and their interpretations. The Ancient Egyptians believed so strongly about the power of dreams to foretell the future and offer advice, that they had rituals to incubate their dreams, and in some cases, they would actually bring their dreams to a special oracle who would further study it.

From other readings, I have discovered that Egyptians created their own Dream Book which is currently part of the archives at the British Museum in London. The Egyptian 'Dream Book' is preserved in the form of a papyrus with a hieratic script. This

208

papyrus was found in the ancient Egyptian workers' village of Deir el-Medina, near the Valley of the Kings. This papyrus has been dated to the early reign of Ramesses II (1279-1213 B.C.). Each page of the papyrus begins with a vertical column of hieratic signs which translates as 'If a man sees himself in a dream'. In each horizontal line that follows, a dream is described, and the diagnosis 'good' or 'bad', as well as the interpretation is provided. The 'Dream Book' has been demonstrated to be an heirloom that was handed down from one generation to the next.

The **Bible – Old Testament** contains many stories about God speaking to leaders, seers and prophets through dreams. Like many other cultures in the region, the ancient Hebrews believed that sleep **thinned the veil** between the living world and the world of demons, angels and spirits, and that sometimes, God himself spoke to humans through their dreams.

One of the most famous stories of dream interpretation from the Bible is that of Joseph, who was sold into slavery by his brothers because he told them his dreams — and who then became one of Egypt's most powerful men because he interpreted the dreams of the Pharaoh and saved the land from famine.

Jean-Marie Husser, a professor of religious history at the University of Strasbourg, notes that the people of the Old Testament world viewed dreams as a "recognized means of access to divine wisdom," and cites the stories of Joseph, Samuel, Daniel and Balaam as examples.

In his 1994 book, "*Walking the Sky: Visionary Traditions of the Great Plains*," Lee Irwin delved deep into the spiritual significance of dreams and visions among the cultures of **Native American nations** of the American Midwest. Like many other ancient peoples, many Native American cultures viewed the dream space as a sacred place, one where a person could step outside the bonds of mundane existence and connect with a more universal consciousness.

Irwin is careful to point out that there are distinct and important differences in the spiritual practices and beliefs of various Indian nations, but also that they share many similarities. Most specifically, there is a shared appreciation of the dream space as a sacred, holy place to be attained through ritual activities.

This author's other readings found that the first business of the day in an Iroquois village (a NY Indian nation) was dream sharing, as dreams were messages from the spirits and the deeper self, and might contain guidance for the community.

The early Iroquois (included Seneca, Cayuga, Onondaga, Oneida and Mohawk Indian tribes) believed that, in dreams, we routinely travel beyond the body and the limits of time and space. They believed that they could visit the future or the past, and enter the realms of the departed and of spiritual teachers.

In **Australian Aboriginal** mythology, the ancestral spirits dreamed the world, including their own forms, into existence. The aboriginal name for this period of creation—common across many dialects and languages—loosely translates as Dreamtime, or The Dreaming.

In these special dreams, they could meet and talk with ancestral spirits, or witness creation as it happened. Dreaming was a way of connecting with the ancestral spirits of the land, of learning about the world and of keeping the Dreamtime alive.

The article titled: *The History and Meaning of Dreams in Ancient Cultures* – January 13, 2011 by Ann Faraday (https://blog.snoozester.com), discusses the meaning of dreams from various countries and cultures. I will summarize her article, quoting where necessary to deliver the writer's exact words.

'*People have been fascinated by dreams for thousands of years and cultures around the world have developed their own traditions for interpreting dreams*'.

Earliest information about dreams comes from Mesopotamia (the land between the Tigris and Euphrates – part of what is now Iraq). The civilization that existed there around 5,000 BC created what is believed to be the world's first book of dreams which was a compilation of dream symbols and their meanings.

Sumerians viewed their dreams as **Signs** from gods, and people had dreams translated by 'dream priests' who foretold the dreamer's future. It is speculated that the process of incubating dreams and summoning them by means of special rituals was invented during this period.

In ancient **Rome**, the tradition of dream interpretation was largely drawn from the Greeks. Augustus, the successor of Julius Cesar, believed so strongly in the prophetic nature of dreams that he created a law requiring every citizen who had a dream about the empire, to talk about it at the market in their town.

In Rome, the importance of dreams was a topic often discussed among scholars who openly proclaimed that dreams are inspired by our passions, emotions and experiences of everyday life and do not come from gods.

In the Middle Ages, dreams were often seen as a way to communicate with the devil and were often associated with witchcraft and sorcery. Many people believed that dreams were a way to gain access to the spiritual world and that they were a source of evil and temptation.

'For millennia, people have sought help with understanding and interpreting dreams; it is believed that by doing so we could gain wisdom and find solutions to our problems'. <end of article>

With the scientific method, developed during the Renaissance, the study of dreams took a more scientific approach. The famous scientist and philosopher René Descartes believed that dreams were a result of the brain's activity and were not a source of spiritual guidance or communication.

212

In the 20th century, the study of dreams took on a more psychological approach with the development of Freudian theory. Sigmund Freud believed that dreams were a way to access the unconscious mind and that they were a reflection of our innermost thoughts, desires, and conflicts.

Today, the study of dreams is a multi-disciplinary field, with researchers from fields such as psychology, neuroscience, and biology. And while we still have much to learn about the nature of dreams, modern science has provided us with a deeper understanding of the function and purpose of dreams.

For me, dreams have presented Signs of the departed who wanted to pass along a message and to offer peace and comfort. However, I too cannot discount that dreams may be mere reflections of our otherwise daily experiences.

Being a frequent participant on social media I found the following story on Facebook, though it's unclear who the original author is.

I arrived at the address and honked the horn. After waiting a few minutes, I honked again. I thought about just driving away, but instead I put the car in park and walked up to the door and knocked... 'Just a minute', answered a frail, elderly voice. I could hear something being dragged across the floor.

After a long pause, the door opened. A small woman in her 90's stood before me. She was wearing a print dress and a pillbox hat with a veil pinned on it, like somebody out of a 1940's movie.

By her side was a small nylon suitcase. The apartment looked
as if no one had lived in it for years. All the furniture was covered
with sheets. There were no clocks on the walls, no knickknacks
or utensils on the counters. In the corner was a cardboard box
filled with photos and glassware.

'Would you carry my bag out to the car?' she said. I took the
suitcase to the cab, then returned to assist the woman. She
took my arm and we walked slowly toward the curb.

She kept thanking me for my kindness. 'It's nothing', I told her...
'I just try to treat my passengers the way I would want my mother
to be treated.' 'Oh, you're such a good boy,' she said.

When we got in the cab, she gave me an address and then
asked, 'Could you drive through downtown?' 'It's not the
shortest way,' I answered quickly... 'Oh, I don't mind,' she said.
'I'm in no hurry. I'm on my way to a hospice.'

I looked in the rear-view mirror. Her eyes were glistening. 'I don't
have any family left,' she continued in a soft voice... 'The doctor
says I don't have very long.' I quietly reached over and shut off
the meter. 'What route would you like me to take?' I asked.

For the next two hours, we drove through the city. She showed
me the building where she had once worked as an elevator
operator. We drove through the neighborhood where she and
her husband had lived when they were newlyweds. She had me

214

pull up in front of a furniture warehouse that had once been a ballroom where she had gone dancing as a girl.

Sometimes she'd ask me to slow in front of a particular building or corner and would sit staring into the darkness, saying nothing. As the first hint of sun was creasing the horizon, she suddenly said, 'I'm tired. Let's go now'.

We drove in silence to the address she had given me. It was a low building, like a small convalescent home, with a driveway that passed under a portico.

Two orderlies came out to the cab as soon as we pulled up. They were solicitous and intent, watching her every move. They must have been expecting her. I opened the trunk and took the small suitcase to the door. The woman was already seated in a wheelchair.

'How much do I owe you?' She asked, reaching into her purse. 'Nothing,' I said. 'You have to make a living,' she answered. 'There are other passengers,' I responded. Almost without thinking, I bent and gave her a hug. She held onto me tightly. 'You gave an old woman a little moment of joy,' she said. 'Thank you.'

I squeezed her hand, and then walked into the dim morning light. Behind me, a door shut. It was the sound of the closing of a life.

The end of the story went on to tell how the cab driver felt from the experience. However, I took another meaning from the reading of the story. This dying woman with no other family around, knowing her days were numbered, wanted to relive her past, by visiting the town and seeing it one last time through what were once youthful eyes. This left the woman comforted and in some ways at peace and it's that same feeling that has been reported by many through the Visitation Dreams that I have discussed. Perhaps that is why this story resonated with me.

I realize this is a story, perhaps real, perhaps not, and written to give the reader a sense of reality of just what your gestures, perhaps simple gestures, may mean to others. I view this in the same manner for which I have viewed my Signs. My brother's device sounding Stupid Jerk not long after he passed was a sign to me of his being there, still, and with a joke to let me know he was doing well. My mom coming to me in my dream with the words 'Not Enough' still giving me pause as to their exact meaning, but at the same time a Sign that mom was still here, and in her way sending me a message as best she could.

It's important to know that Signs are all about us once we begin to realize it. Though I would be remiss if I did not say, not all happenings are Signs. Sometimes they are coincidences or are just day to day living experiences, and sometimes they are the conveyance of so much more that we need to pay attention to.

For as you begin to explore your own signs you may find that indeed the Veil is thinner than we imagine.

REFERENCES

Reference material and sources are listed below by the chapter where they were referenced and utilized.

Preface:

The Five Man Electrical Band is a Canadian rock band from Ottawa, Ontario. They had many hits and are best known for their 1971 hit single "Signs".

Movie: **Tommy Boy** – is a 1995 American buddy comedy film directed by Peter Segal, written by Bonnie and Terry Turner, produced by Lorne Michaels, and starring former Saturday Night Live castmates and close friends Chris Farley and David Spade.

The Third Man Factor – Surviving the Impossible – by John Geiger (book) is a theory of how people, in many critical situations, or at the very edge of death often sense an unseen presence offering hope, protection, and guidance. These spirit guardians encourage individuals, under extreme circumstances, to make a final effort to survive.

https://www.dailywire.com/news/olivia-newton-johns-family-talks-supernatural-encounters-with-late-star-in-year-after-her-death

Intro:
https://www.hospicebuffalo.com/

Chapter 1

1.1 Movie: **On a Wing and a Prayer** – is a 2023 American biographical survival film directed by Sean McNamara and starring Dennis Quaid, Heather Graham, and Jesse Metcalfe. It was released on April 7, 2023 which was Good Friday.
1.1 9/11 Twin Towers collapse timeline:
https://www.nps.gov/flni/learn/historyculture/september-11-2001-timeline.htm
Todd Beamer UA flight 93 and Let's Roll:
https://en.wikipedia.org/wiki/Todd_Beamer
1.3 Doug White and the King Air N559DW story: Archie Safety Award Ceremony

https://www.bing.com/videos/riverview/relatedvideo?
&q=archie+league+medal+ceremony&&mid=09E69A81ACAB0E
A40EF709E69A81ACAB0EA40EF7&&FORM=VRDGAR
1.3 February 8, 2023 Religious event at Ashbury College in
Wilmore, Kentucky – The Ashbury Outpouring:
https://www.asbury.edu/outpouring/
1.4 Navy Admiral William H. McRaven, at the University-Wide
Commencement – University of Texas at Austin, May 17,
2014https://news.utexas.edu/2014/05/16/mcraven-urges-
graduates-to-find-courage-to-change-the-world/
1.4 Jason McElwain (J-Mac) Senior's Night basketball game.
https://www.youtube.com/watch?v=1fw1CcxCUgg
https://en.wikipedia.org/wiki/Jason_McElwain
https://www.espn.com/espn/story/_/id/14780896/jason-mcelwain-
changed-lives-inspired-autistic-community-20-point-game-10-
years-ago

Chapter 2

2.1 and 6.0 – Book: *Death is but a dream* – Finding Hope and
Meaning at Life's End – by Christopher Kerr, MD, PHD, with
Caroline Mardorossian, PHD
2.2 The Compassionate Friends supports families after the loss
of a child at any age. https://www.compassionatefriends.org/

Chapter 3:

3.4 Redbird Candies: https://redbirdcandies.com

Chapter 5:

5.1 Signs from Heaven ... 9 Signs from Deceased Loved Ones –
https://www.ask-angels.com/spiritual-guidance/signs-from-
heaven/
5.1 Visited by a Hummingbird? What does it mean spiritually? –
https://crystalclearintuition.com/hummingbird-spiritual-meaning/
5.2 Egyptian Dream Book
(https://www.ancient-origins.net/myths-legends/egyptian-dream-
book-001621)
5.2https://en.wikipedia.org/wiki/The_Hitchhiker
%27s_Guide_to_the_Galaxy
5.2 https://www.scientificamerican.com/article/for-math-fans-a-
hitchhikers-guide-to-the-number-42/
5.2 https://www.ryanhart.org/number-1234-meaning/

5.2 https://numerologist.com/numerology/why-you-see-angel-number-123/
5.2 https://www.cnn.com/2023/01/03/us/damar-hamlin-bills-nfl-response-timeline/index.html#Hamlin%20%E2%80%98Promptly%20Resuscitated%E2%80%99%20on%20The%20Field
5.3 https://www.foxnews.com/lifestyle/what-are-angel-numbers-why-people-keep-seeing-them

Chapter 6:

6.0 Video DVD: **Death is but a dream** – a film by J.J. Sicotte & Monica De La Torre; video of Dr Kerr and his patients at Hospice and Palliative Care Center, Buffalo NY
6.0 I See Dead People: Dreams and Visions of the Dying | Dr. Christopher Kerr | TEDx Buffalo
https://www.bing.com/videos/riverview/relatedvideo?&q=Ingrid+Spilde+with+Dr.+Christopher+Kerr&mid=191F5AF6FFFFEB4F2C98191F5AF6FFFFEB4F2C98&ajaxhist=0

Dr. Kerr website www.drchristopherkerr.com
Netflix special called: Surviving Death (Dr Kerr is in Episode 5)

PBS special called: Death is but a Dream

6.0
https://www.psychologytoday.com/us/blog/dream-catcher/201806/visitation-dreams-ii-dreams-the-bereaved
https://floatingintheblue.blogspot.com/2012/04/thin-places-biblical-investigation.html

Appendix
Appendix 2: Article: The Impact of Dreams of the Deceased on Bereavement: A Survey of Hospice Caregivers – by Scott T. Wright, BA, Christopher Kerr, Md, PHD, Nicole M. Doroszczuk, LMSW, Sarah M. Kuszczak, BS, Pei C. Hang, PHD, and Debra L. Luczkiewicz, MD

Appendix 3 https://dreamstudies.org/how-dreams-of-bereavement-reach-out-to-us/
Appendix 3 https://dreamtending.com/blog/what-do-dreams-mean-ancient-cultures/

Appendix 3 https://blog.snoozester.com/history-and-meaning-of-dreams-in-ancient-cultures/

"Relax, you're on a journey of discovery. Let life reveal itself to you."
Melody Beattie

ACKNOWLEDGEMENT

I wish to thank several people for their contributions to this book as I am deeply grateful and hope I have done them all justice with the writing of their personal stories.

- Mr. Brian Clark and Mr. Ron DiFrancesco, incredible survivors of the South Tower collapse on 9/11, and whose remarkable journeys on that fateful day are truly miraculous.
- Dr. Christopher Kerr, head of Hospice and Palliative Care Center, Buffalo, NY, whose compassion has made it his life's work to aid in the peaceful transition that many in Hospice have experienced on their own journey into the next realm.
- Mr. Doug White, Mr. Kari Sorenson and his fiancé Ms. Ashley Harrison whose story has been retold in the movie – **On a Wing and a Prayer** – a true story about the remarkable landing of a King Air airplane on Easter Sunday 2009 after the original pilot fell dead shortly after takeoff.
- Coach Jim Johnson whose action on a high school basketball team's Senior Night, allowing the basketball team's student assistant manager, Jason McElwain (J-Mac) who is autistic, to suit up and take the court with a little over four minutes left in the game and J-Mac's remarkable performance that followed.

- Mr. Ed Currie and his story of just wanting to stop the pain of his addiction. Then after seeing the angelic vision, going through rehab and who is today sober, with a family and a thriving pepper business. One that is recognized by the Guiness Book of World Records for having created the world's hottest pepper.
- And to my dear friends and family who have been so generous to share their stories with me: Marjorie (Boofie) Longley Graham, my daughter and son-in-law Jen and Jason, my daughter-in-law Julie, my sister Diane, and my wife Sharon.

And for the readers of this book, I wish you all much success on your own personal journey of discovery and the finding of the meaning for the Signs that may be present in your own lives! May you find solace in recognizing and interpreting those Signs.

"Confronting our feelings and giving them appropriate expression always takes strength, not weakness". – Fred Rogers a.k.a. Mr. Roger's of Mr. Rogers Neighborhood.

Though Mr. Rogers was referring to the feelings of 'Anger', I feel the sentiment can be viewed to encompass most all of our feelings, including our feelings for the unknown.

INDEX

"Mystery creates wonder and wonder is the basis of man's desire to understand." Neil Armstrong

I truly hope you enjoyed reading this book, and if you did, there is no better compliment to an author than a positive book review.

Positive reviews help the book rank better on the platform that sells them, and this helps spread the word by giving potential readers insight about the books content.

Plus, a review creates good karma, and who couldn't use a little good karma.

If you are having your own SIGN stories and wish to share them, my contact information is located at kevin-hall.com. Thank you so very much.

Kevin M. Hall

www.ingramcontent.com/pod-product-compliance
Lightning Source LLC
Chambersburg PA
CBHW020444130626
46549CB00001B/297